Signification and Significance

STUDIES IN COMMUNICATION

EDITORS

Leo L. Beranek　　　*Roman Jakobson*　　　*William N. Locke*

SIGNIFICATION AND SIGNIFICANCE: A STUDY OF THE RELATIONS OF SIGNS AND VALUES
By Charles Morris

THOUGHT AND LANGUAGE
By L. S. Vygotsky

WORD AND OBJECT
By Willard Van Orman Quine

ON HUMAN COMMUNICATION: A REVIEW, A SURVEY, AND A CRITICISM
By Colin Cherry

Signification and Significance

A STUDY OF THE RELATIONS OF SIGNS AND VALUES

Charles Morris

The M.I.T. Press
Massachusetts Institute of Technology
Cambridge, Massachusetts

Copyright © 1964 by
The Massachusetts Institute of Technology
All Rights Reserved

Library of Congress Catalog Card Number: 64-22212
Printed in the United States of America

ISBN 0-262-63014-1 (paperback)

The object of symbolism is the enhancement of the importance of what is symbolized.
—ALFRED NORTH WHITEHEAD

The study of the modes of language becomes, as it attempts to be thorough, the most fundamental and extensive of all inquiries.
—I. A. RICHARDS

The symbol may, with Emerson's sphynx, say to man, Of thine eye, I am eyebeam.
—CHARLES SANDERS PEIRCE

Preface

For several decades my work has centered around two problems: the development of a general theory of signs and the development of a general theory of value. *Signs, Language, and Behavior* was the product of the first concern, and *Varieties of Human Value* was a product of the second. Both problems were approached in terms of the theory of action or behavior developed in its essentials by George H. Mead.

The present study is an attempt to bring together these two lines of development. It was begun in 1956–1957 during a year's stay at the Center for Advanced Study in the Behavioral Sciences.

That there are close relations between the terms 'signification' and 'significance' is evident. In many languages there is a term like the English term 'meaning' which has two poles: that which something signifies and the value or significance of what is signified. Thus if we ask what is the meaning of life, we may be asking a question about the signification of the term 'life', or asking a question about the value or significance of living—or both. The fact that such terms as 'meaning' are so widespread in many languages (with the polarity mentioned) suggests that there is a basic relation between what we shall distinguish as *signification* and *significance*. The nature of signification and significance, as well as their relations within human behavior, is the subject matter of this book.

I shall in the nature of the case draw heavily upon my earlier work in these areas. A knowledge of this work is, however, not required by the reader. The book also contains some relatively important changes in my former views, and considerable material not previously presented. The book thus gives me a chance to rethink my ideas in these areas, and to present a more integrated formulation of the relations of signification and significance within human behavior.

Many years of work have been motivated by the conviction that a new and important outlook on the nature of man is emerging, and that this outlook will be clarified greatly as we come to understand better the ways in which signs and values function in human life.

This book is not technical enough or comprehensive enough to give much aid to the professional philosopher or to solve in detail the specific problems of value of the behavioral scientists. It is a framework for viewing these matters. I hope that it will be relevant to those interested in the relations of signs, values, and behavior.

I am grateful for help in the preparation of this book given by a succession of graduate research assistants: Dr. Denis O'Donovan, Mr. Frank N. Sciadini, Mr. Fred R. Berger, Mr. Daniel J. Hamilton, and Mr. B. Wayne Shirbroun. Mrs. Evelyn Weight was responsible for the final typing of the work.

The book owes much to the students in my seminars at the University of Florida during the last five years. I thank Professor George R. Bartlett and the University of Florida for making available the time needed to do this work.

CHARLES MORRIS

Gainesville, Florida
December 25, 1963

Contents

CHAPTER 1. *Signs and the Act*

1.	The Scope of Semiotic	1
2.	The Basic Terms of Semiotic	2
3.	Dimensions of Signification	3
4.	Interpretants	6
5.	Summary of the Analysis	7
6.	The Terms 'Meaning' and 'Express'	9
7.	Formal Signs	11
8.	Formative Discourse	13
9.	The Uses of Signs	14

CHAPTER 2. *Values, Signs, and the Act*

1.	The Concept of Value	16
2.	Values and Preferential Behavior	17
3.	Operative, Conceived, and Object Values	19
4.	Three Aspects of Systems	20
5.	The Primary Values and Signs	21
6.	Individual and Social Forms of the Primary Values	23
7.	Signs, Values, and Inquiry	26
8.	Evaluative versus Nonevaluative Inquiry	28
9.	Mead and Certain Features of Human Mentality	29

Contents

CHAPTER 3. *Semiotic and Some Issues in Contemporary Philosophy*

    1. The Philosopher's Concern with Language   32
    2. Axiology and "the Naturalistic Fallacy"   34
    3. The Ought and the Is   36
    4. The Cognitivist-Emotivist Controversy   38
    5. The Absolutist-Relativist Controversy   41
    6. Semiotic, Axiology, and Philosophy   43
    7. Philosophy and Pragmatics   44
    8. Concluding Words   47

CHAPTER 4. *Semiotic, Axiology, and the Behavioral Sciences*

    1. The Problem   49
    2. The Nature of the Interpretant   49
    3. Dimensionality and the Semantic Differential   52
    4. Osgood's Factors and the Kinds of Interpretants   54
    5. Semiotic, Axiology, and the Social Sciences   56
    6. A Note Concerning Contemporary Linguistics   60
    7. A Note Concerning Information Theory   62

CHAPTER 5. *Art, Signs, and Values*

    1. The Issues   65
    2. One Approach to These Issues   66
    3. The Aesthetic Sign as an Icon   68
    4. The Aesthetic Sign and Values   69
    5. Art as the Embodiment or Portrayal of Values   70
    6. Supplementary Approaches   72
    7. Experimental Possibilities   73
    8. Experimental Studies   74
    9. Some Further Considerations   77
   10. Art and Human Behavior   79

CHAPTER 6. *Signs, Values, and Personality Disturbances*   81

    Bibliography   88

    Index   97

Signification and Significance

1

Signs and the Act

§ 1. THE SCOPE OF SEMIOTIC

SEMIOTIC has for its goal a general theory of signs in all their forms and manifestations, whether in animals or men, whether normal or pathological, whether linguistic or nonlinguistic, whether personal or social. Semiotic is thus an interdisciplinary enterprise.

Part of the widespread interest in this area is motivated by the belief that higher-level sign processes (often called symbols) are of central importance in understanding man and his works. Ernst Cassirer called man "the symbolic animal" (*"animal symbolicum"*), instead of "the rational animal" (*"animal rationale"*), and much contemporary work has shown the aptness of this conception.

The term 'semiotic' was adapted by John Locke from the Greek Stoics, who in turn were influenced by the Greek medical tradition that interpreted diagnosis and prognosis as sign processes. Charles S. Peirce (1839–1914), who followed John Locke's usage, is responsible for the present widespread employment of the term 'semiotic'. The terms 'significs' and 'semantics' are also in use, though the tendency now is to use 'semantics' for only one branch of semiotic.

Philosophers and linguists made the main historical contributions to the general theory of signs, but today extensive work in this area is also being done by psychologists, psychiatrists, aestheticians, sociologists, and anthropologists.

§ 2. THE BASIC TERMS OF SEMIOTIC

For present purposes the basic terms of semiotic can be introduced as follows: Semiosis (or sign process) is regarded as a five-term relation—v, w, x, y, z—in which v sets up in w the disposition to react in a certain kind of way, x, to a certain kind of object, y (not then acting as a stimulus), under certain conditions, z. The v's, in the cases where this relation obtains, are *signs*, the w's are *interpreters*, the x's are *interpretants*, the y's are *significations*, and the z's are the *contexts* in which the signs occur.

Karl von Frisch[1] has shown that a bee which finds nectar is able, on returning to the hive, to "dance" in such a way as to direct other bees to the food source. In this case the dance is the sign; the other bees affected by the dance are interpreters; the disposition to react in a certain kind of way by these bees, because of the dance,[2] is the interpretant; the kind of object toward which the bees are prepared to act in this way is the signification of the sign; and the position of the hive is part of the context.

Concerning this formulation of semiosis (or sign process, or sign behavior) several comments are in order.

First, the formulation is not proposed as a definition of 'sign', for there may be things we shall want to call signs that do not meet the requirements of this formulation—I prefer to leave this an open question. The formulation simply gives the conditions for recognizing certain events as signs.

Second, to say that what is signified is not at the moment a stimulus is not to deny that we may signify objects present in immediate experience—as in pointing to the desk upon which I am writing and saying "That is a desk." For 'desk' signifies an object with a rear, an underside, drawers that can be pulled out, etc.—none of which are at the present moment available to my observation. Only some aspects of the desk are directly observed.

Third, while this formulation is behavioral, and such sign behavior is open to objective study, an organism may experience

---

[1] Karl von Frisch, *Bees, Their Vision, Chemical Senses, and Language* (Ithaca, New York: Cornell University Press, 1950).

[2] Note the qualification, since not all dispositions occur in sign processes. Independent of signs, there are many dispositions to respond in certain ways to certain things.

and, in the case of human beings at least, may report on its own sign behavior. Nevertheless, a behavioral formulation is more basic than a self-observational formulation, since semiotic must deal with sign processes in animals, in children prior to the acquisition of language, and in personality disturbances where self-observational reports are absent or unreliable. Self-observational reports on sign processes are, however, not ruled out by a behavioral semiotic, since they are themselves a kind of sign behavior.

Fourth, I see no objection to introducing "significations" in this way. They are not "entities" in any objectionable sense, but certain describable aspects of complex behavioral processes in the natural world. As such they can be talked about without being "reified." That the bees are disposed by the dance to seek food objects in a certain context can be observed, just as in other contexts the dance serves to send the bees to explore certain locations as possible sites for a new hive. There is nothing "mythical" about significations when so interpreted.[3]

Fifth, the context in which something functions as a sign may include other signs, but need not do so.

Sixth, the interpretant, as a disposition to react in a certain way because of the sign (food-seeking behavior or site-probing behavior in the case of bees), has no necessarily "subjective" connotation. Such a disposition can, if one wishes, be interpreted in probabilistic terms, as the probability of reacting in a certain way under certain conditions because of the appearance of the sign. Or, as we shall see later, it can be interpreted as an intervening variable, postulated for theoretical purposes, and controllable by indirect empirical evidence.

§ 3. DIMENSIONS OF SIGNIFICATION

It is widely recognized that signs which are commonly (but not universally) admitted to have signification differ greatly in the kind of signification they have. 'Black', 'good', and 'ought' are obvious examples. There are, however, many ways in which such differences are accounted for.

---

[3] My earlier formulations led to certain objections on this score. See my review of B. F. Skinner's *Verbal Behavior*, under the title "Words Without Meaning," in *Contemporary Psychology* 3 (1958), pp. 212-214.

My suggestion is that signification is tridimensional, and that these three dimensions are explicable in terms of three phases or aspects of action. I shall follow George H. Mead's analysis of an act.[4]

According to Mead, if an impulse (as a disposition to a certain kind of action) is given, the resulting action has three phases: the perceptual, the manipulatory, and the consummatory. The organism must perceive the relevant features of the environment in which it is to act; it must behave toward these objects in a way relevant to the satisfaction of its impulse; and if all goes well, it then attains the phase of activity which is the consummation of the act. Since act and object are correlative in his account, Mead also speaks of the distance properties of the object, its manipulatory properties, and its consummatory properties.

Now, if signs are treated behaviorally, it may be that their significations are related to these three aspects of action and so exhibit tridimensionality. It is proposed that every sign be regarded as having three dimensions, though some signs will be strongest on certain dimensions, and in some cases they will have a null weighting on certain dimensions.

A sign is *designative* insofar as it signifies *observable*[5] properties of the environment or of the actor, it is *appraisive* insofar as it signifies the consummatory properties of some object or situation, and it is *prescriptive* insofar as it signifies how the object or situation is to be reacted to so as to satisfy the governing impulse. In these terms, usually 'black' is primarily designative, 'good' is

---

[4] George Herbert Mead, *The Philosophy of the Act*, Charles W. Morris, ed., with the collaboration of John M. Brewster, Albert M. Dunham, and David L. Miller (Chicago: University of Chicago Press, 1938).

[5] The term 'observable' is here employed in a fairly narrow sense: "observable directly by sense organs or indirectly by the observation of events which have been observed to act as evidence for events not observable directly by sense organs." The term 'observation' has a wide range of application in the everyday language, and some thinkers will want to dispense with the term in this context, so that semiotic will not seem to set arbitrary limits to the range of signification of signs. Major philosophical views hang upon what are taken to be the limits of signification. These views cannot be discussed in this preliminary formulation. Attention may be called to the analysis of the phases of the referential function of language, in Willard Van Orman Quine's *Word and Object* (Cambridge, Mass: The Technology Press of the Massachusetts Institute of Technology; New York: John Wiley & Sons, 1960), pp. 108-110.

primarily appraisive, and 'ought' is primarily prescriptive. It should of course be recognized that context is always relevant, so that in some contexts 'black' may be primarily appraisive or prescriptive, 'good' primarily designative or prescriptive, and 'ought' primarily designative or appraisive. One cannot tell from the mere inspection of an uttered or written word its strength on the three dimensions. This requires the study of specific action in a specific situation.

Nevertheless, there is some evidence that certain terms do have signification on the three dimensions,[6] and that there is some agreement as to their relative strengths on these dimensions. In three of my seminars, students were given the form 'X is ─────', and were told that X was a man. They were then told successively that X was humble, proud, hard, wet, wise, severe, objective, kind, serious, cowardly, and old, and were asked to assign a percentage to each sentence indicating to what extent it was designative, appraisive, and prescriptive. In general, there was considerable agreement in the three groups as to whether a given sentence was, in this context, predominantly designative, appraisive, or prescriptive. Thus all groups thought of 'cowardly' as having considerable strength on all three dimensions, but most strength on the appraisive dimension; and they all thought of 'old' as primarily designative. These results are not scientifically impressive, but at any rate they indicate that experimental studies in this area are possible.

In relation to Mead's analysis of the act, the expectation would be for designative signs to be predominant in the perceptual stage of the act, for here the actor is seeking to obtain information concerning the situation in which he is acting. In the manipulatory stage of action it seems plausible that the signs involved would be primarily prescriptive, signifying how the object or situation is to be reacted to. In the consummatory phase of action, the

---

[6] Some readers will object to the use of the term 'dimension' in this connection, and they may prefer such terms as 'factor' and 'respect'. The semiotic "dimensions" are not dimensions in the strictest mathematical sense (as are the value dimensions of Chapter 2). But the values of the variables are partly independent, and while no scale is known which is common to all of them, the values of each dimension are to some extent quantifiable.

signs involved would be primarily appraisive, signifying the consummatory properties of the object or situation.

§ 4. INTERPRETANTS

Since on the present model all signs have interpretants, different kinds of interpretants would occur for the three dimensions of signification. The interpretant of a sign is a disposition to react in a certain kind of way because of the sign. Corresponding to the designative dimension of signification, the interpretant would be a disposition to react to the designated object as if it had certain observable properties. Thus if one is told that there is a black object in an adjoining room, one is set for certain visual experiences on entering the room.

In the case of appraisive signs, the interpretant would be a disposition to act toward a designated object as if it would be satisfying or unsatisfying. Thus if a mother tries to get her child to swallow a teaspoonful of castor oil by saying "nummy num," the child is set for something that he will favor. Since he does not like it when he tastes it, and if the mother continues to talk like this in a variety of situations, the term 'nummy num' will change from a positive appraisive sign to a negative appraisive sign—or the child will come to regard his mother as a liar.

In the case of primarily prescriptive signs the interpretant would be a disposition to act in a certain kind of way to the designated object or situation. If a person trying unsuccessfully to open a door is told that he ought to press down on the knob, he is disposed to perform that kind of atcion and in most cases to expect that in so performing it he will be able to get out of the room.

It is especially notable that any given sign may in varying degrees operate in all the dimensions of signification, and hence have all the corresponding interpretant dimensions. The sentence "He is a coward" may illustrate this.[7] Terms like 'black', 'good', and 'ought' are simply cases where certain dimensions of signification and certain kinds of interpretant are predominant. More will be said of such terms later.

---

[7] See John Dewey's analysis of 'cowardly' and 'friendly', in *Experience and Nature* (Chicago: Open Court Publishing Co., 1925), pp. 292-293.

§ 5. SUMMARY OF THE ANALYSIS

For the moment let us shift the focus of our attention from the phases of action in Mead's sense to certain general requirements of action. Three requirements will be discussed.

The actor must obtain information concerning the situation in which he is to act, he must select among objects that he will favor or accord positive preferential behavior, and he must act on the selected object by some specific course of behavior. Thus if he is thirsty and finds that tea and coffee are available, he must act preferentially to one of these—say tea—and he must decide whether to drink the tea quickly or slowly, alone or with a companion, and so forth.

These three requirements of action are common to all action, nonhuman and human, and may take place without signs, or with signs at the prelinguistic level, or with linguistic signs in a complex process of inquiry. The behavior of an amoeba may be at the first level, the warning cry of a duck to her ducklings at the second level, and considerable human behavior at the third level. Inquiry will be considered at some length later. Here it need only be noted that appraisive signs operative in inquiry are signs of possible consummatory objects, while appraisive signs at the consummatory phase of the act report on the direct experience of consummation or frustration. The tea appraised in inquiry as nummy-num may or may not be called nummy-num when tasted.

Some of the results of the preceding analysis, in somewhat different terms, are presented in Table 1. The terminology of the interpretant column perhaps needs no elaboration. A possible hypothesis is that the interpretant of primarily designative signs strongly involves (among other things) the sensory nervous system including the sensory projection areas of the cortex, that primarily appraisive signs strongly involve the autonomic nervous system including the memory sections and pleasure centers, and that primarily prescriptive signs strongly involve the somatic (or motor) nervous system including the effector system of the brain. This suggestion of course does not deny that in all cases other aspects of the organism are operative, and since most signs actually

Table 1. Signs and Action Requirements

Action Requirements	Dimensions of Signification	Interpretant (Disposition to Respond by):	Significations
1. Obtaining information	Designative	Sense organs	Stimulus properties of object
2. Selection of objects for preferential behavior	Appraisive	Object preferences	Reinforcing properties of object
3. Action on object by specific behavior	Prescriptive	Behavior preferences	Act as instrumental

have weights on all three dimensions of signification, it does not imply that the interpretant of a sign is limited to one aspect of nervous activity and its related organic accompaniments. But it does suggest that the tridimensionality of signification is reflected in a tridimensionality of interpretants.

The terminology in the significations column is borrowed from psychology, and it needs some explication. 'Stimulus property' is used here in a wide sense. It includes not merely the characteristics of the object which activate a sense organ but those which might do so under certain conditions (such as on the other side of the moon), and even those properties which though not themselves observable can affect an instrument which is observable (such as the temperature at the surface of the sun). Thus the range of designation is much wider than what can be directly observed.

By 'reinforcing property of an object' is meant the capacity of an object to increase the probability of the performance of a response made to it. Thus when certain kinds of food are tasted by a dog, he will eat them; but when others are tasted, they are spurned. The first kind of food is said to have a reinforcing property, and the second kind of food not to have it. Although such properties are not additional stimulus properties, I see no objection to speaking of them as properties of an object. It is true that they are properties of an object only in relation to an organism, so that an object which has reinforcing properties for the behavior of a dog may not have such properties for the behavior of a cat.

But this is a common situation: we do not hesitate to say that some objects are edible and some are not, though the classification is relative to various kinds of digestive systems. Such properties may be said to be "objectively relative."

To call an act "instrumental" signifies that its performance permits the performance of some other act which an organism is disposed to perform. Thus a hungry animal may get food in an experimental situation if and only if it presses a lever. The act of pressing a lever is then instrumental. The act of pressing down on the doorknob in our earlier example is instrumental to the disposition to get out of the room.

§ 6. THE TERMS 'MEANING' AND 'EXPRESS'

The terms 'meaning' and 'express' have not been introduced as basic terms for semiotic, since they have such a variety of significations and are used in such a variety of ways that it is best not to employ them as basic terms for discussions in this area. But it is of course possible, if one wishes, to introduce them in terms of more basic semiotical terms. Thus it might be said that the "meaning" of a sign is *both* its signification and its interpretant, and neither alone.

In that case merely to say that a certain object has reinforcing properties is not to make an appraisive utterance (i.e., to say something which has appraisive "meaning"). The term 'good', for instance, would therefore have appraisive meaning only if it not merely signified an object as having reinforcing properties but also aroused in its interpreters a disposition to positive preferential behavior toward the object signified. A dietician may say to his patient (perhaps a diabetic) that diet A is good and diet B is bad without inducing in himself a disposition to eat in manner A rather than in manner B—the term 'good' is for him then primarily designative, while for his patient, insofar as it disposes him to give preference to diet A, the term is appraisive as well (i.e., has appraisive "meaning").[8]

---

[8] The term 'good' may even here have an appraisive component for the dietician: if he becomes diabetic, he may then be disposed to diet A rather than diet B because of what he had previously said to his patient.

Similarly for the term 'ought', in some contexts it is purely designative, and in others it has an appraisive component. It has prescriptive meaning only if it signifies to its interpreter that the act which is prescribed is instrumental and in addition actually disposes its interpreter to perform the act in question. Here, too, the "meaning" of an ought-statement may be different for the utterer and for the person addressed.

In the case of designative "meaning," a sign has such meaning to the degree that the interpreter is disposed to sense-organ activity[9] of a certain kind to a certain kind of object. Many signs have all kinds of "meaning" in various degrees.

As for the term 'express', it could be introduced in the present scheme in at least two ways. One might say that every sign expresses its interpretant, without signifying it. Or one might say that a sign is expressive to the degree that its *production* is itself taken as a sign by an interpreter of some state of its producer.[10] In this case not every sign is actually "expressive" though it is potentially so. Of course, certain signs (such as a cry of alarm) are much more frequently interpreted as expressive in this sense than are other signs, and these are the signs which some persons perhaps intend by their use of 'expressive'. But all signs may be interpreted as expressive in this second sense of the term, and what is expressed is by no means limited to emotions or attitudes. Hence, the identification of 'expressive' with 'emotive' engenders many confusions which the present analysis avoids.

It might be maintained that the analysis of the act followed here is too simple—that it stresses what the actor does in relation to the object and neglects what the object does to the actor.[11] The hungry person not only scans his environment for food objects, manipulates them, and chews them, but the object in turn initiates

---

[9] This must be qualified in terms of the earlier comments made upon the term 'observation'.

[10] Of course, in some cases the interpreter of the sign may also be the producer. Abraham Kaplan calls the sign in this case *self-expressive*. It may be noted that not all signs expressive in the first sense of this term are expressive (or self-expressive) in the second sense of the term. In my *Signs, Language, and Behavior* (New York: Prentice-Hall, 1946; New York: George Braziller, 1955), I proposed to use 'expressive' in the second sense, and I still favor this proposal.

[11] Howard Parsons called this to my attention. He is at present working out what is involved here.

a very complex set of processes in the organism. It seems suggestive to say that this more passive, more "undergoing" aspect of behavior has its own kind of sign functioning, and that such signs are primarily "expressive." This area certainly demands extensive exploration and may throw considerable light on mythic, aesthetic, and religious symbolism.

When the person eats an apple, he does become passive in a sense, and the apple "acts on him." But to signify what occurs seems to be describable in terms of the designative, appraisive, and prescriptive dimensions of signification. The person may designate what happens to him, he may appraise this, and he may then formulate prescriptions as to his future eating behavior. These signs may have "meaning" and be "expressive" in the sense of the previous discussion. But the question is whether such important analysis will also require the introduction of a new dimension of signification.

§ 7. FORMAL SIGNS[12]

So far, no account has been given of what are often called "logical" or "grammatical" or "structural" signs, to which are attributed logical or grammatical or structural signification (or "meaning"). Examples are terms like 'or', parentheses, and the '-ly' in 'He came quickly'.

In *Signs, Language, and Behavior* such items were called "formators," and an attempt was made to give them a fourth dimension of signification—"formative signification." Thus 'or', in some of its occurrences, was said to signify that an otherwise signified situation had the property of alternativity. Of the statement "The apple is on the first or second shelf of the ice box" one might say that it designates no observable property of apple and icebox, and neither appraises them nor prescribes action with respect to them. Hence, if we mean by 'lexical' those terms which designate, appraise, or prescribe, then 'or' in this occurrence would be non-lexical. Since it does seem to signify something about the signified

---

[12] The general reader may omit §§ 7 and 8 without losing the central line of analysis.

situation, it might be said to have another type (or dimension) of signification, "formative" signification.[13]

It now seems worthwhile to explore the possibility of maintaining a tridimensional analysis. One of the reasons for introducing a formative dimension of signification is undoubtedly to have a way of explaining the status of formal logic, mathematics, and grammar. Thus if no fourth formative dimension is introduced, there remains the task within a tridimensional analysis of accounting for these statuses.

One possibility, sometimes held, is to regard formators as simply "auxiliary devices" which themselves have no signification but which influence in determinate ways the signification of the sign combinations in which they appear. They might then be called "synsigns." Thus the word order of 'X hit Y', as contrasted to the word order of 'Y hit X', might be regarded as a synsign in this sense, as determining different significations for the two expressions but without having a signification of its own.

Such an analysis may be sufficient to account for some (and perhaps all) of the vague class of items called formators. But there is another possibility, namely of regarding formators as a rather special class of lexical signs, and hence as being analyzable in terms of designative, appraisive, and prescriptive signification. One version of this possibility would be to regard them as metalinguistic signs signifying the signs they accompany. Thus 'or' in 'P or Q' could be interpreted as signifying (in this case designating) the set of pairs of sentences such that at least one of the sentences in a given pair is true. Parentheses would be regarded as designating the expressions around which they occur and prescribing that these expressions are to be treated in a certain way. It is important to realize that there are relations of signification within the field of signs, and not merely to situations outside this field.

I believe that this approach can be carried quite far. Nevertheless, another version of this possibility is to consider (at least

---

[13] Most contemporary linguists still speak of "structural meaning," "grammatical meaning," "formal meaning," "linguistic meaning," or the like. The assumption of such meaning has been called in question by Noam Chomsky, in *Syntactic Structures* (The Hague: Mouton & Co., 1957).

some) formators not as metalinguistic (in the sense that they explicitly signify other signs) but as being at a higher level than the signs they accompany (i.e., they presuppose these signs without actually signifying them). Thus in the case of 'or' mentioned above, it might be said that 'or' signifies something about the situation signified by the other signs of the combination in which it occurs; it would be a situation of alternativity and would be responded to in such and such a way ("If you don't find the apple on the first shelf, look for it on the second," etc.). This differs from the analysis first suggested in introducing the notion of *levels in the object language,* and by keeping the signification of formators lexical, it does not introduce a fourth dimension of signification.

§ 8. FORMATIVE DISCOURSE

Though a dimension of formative signification is not regarded as necessary, it is still necessary in semiotic to account for such formative discourse as is exemplified by mathematics and formal logic. Thus '$2 + 2 = 4$' differs from '2 quarts of alcohol added to 2 quarts of water give 4 quarts of liquid'. The first sentence is formative (and analytic); the second is lexical (and synthetic). The first is formally true; the second is empirically false. The negatives of these sentences are, respectively, formally false and empirically true.

It is not my concern here to discuss comprehensively the problems of formative discourse. A suggestion, however, may indicate a direction of possible analysis.

The relation of *analytic implicates* between two signs (or sets of signs) can be introduced as follows: Where the signification of S_1 is contained in or is identical with the signification of S_2, then S_2 is an analytic implicate of S_1. Thus in 'Men are animals', 'animals' is an analytic implicate of 'men'. If something is a man, then by the signification of the term 'man' that something is an animal. Similar examples would be found in 'A is A' and 'Black berries are black'. 'Blackberries are black' is not an example of such a formative sentence. It is an empirical sentence, and at an early stage of the growth of blackberries it is in fact false.

The relation of *contradictory implicates* can be introduced as follows: Where the signification of S_1 is the absence of the conditions which constitute the signification of S_2, S_1 and S_2 are said to be contradictory implicates of each other. 'Men are not-men', 'A is not-A', 'Black berries are not-black' are examples of sentences built upon contradictory implicates. By the signification of the signs it is known that if one of the signs applies to something, the other does not; and if one sign does not apply to something, the other one does.

Insofar as discourse is based on analytic implicates, it is analytic formative discourse; and insofar as it is based on contradictory implicates, it is contradictory formative discourse. Mathematical discourse often (or always) is of the former sort, and mystical discourse is often (or always) of the second sort.[14]

It is thus possible within the present framework of semiotic to admit a type of formative (as opposed to lexical) discourse, and yet not to introduce a fourth (formative) dimension of signification over and above the designative, appraisive, and prescriptive dimensions. Hence, we need not complicate the analysis of stages of the act to account for formative discourse.

§ 9. THE USES OF SIGNS

Contemporary analyses of signs stress strongly the many uses of signs, especially linguistic signs. But the terms 'signification', 'use', and 'usage', and their relations are conceived very diversely. Some persons identify the signification of a word with how it is used, and some with its usage. 'Use' and 'usage' are at times distinguished, and at times not.

If pragmatics is concerned with the origin, uses, and effects of signs, then to speak of the "use" of a sign presupposes that it already has a signification. Hence, in this framework 'signification' and 'use' are distinguished. 'Usage of a sign', however, if distinguished from 'use', does not suggest to me anything above

---

[14] See my paper, "Mysticism and Its Language," *Language: An Enquiry into Its Meaning and Function*, Ruth Nanda Anshen, ed. (New York: Harper & Brothers, 1957), pp. 179-187. The paper (in a slightly shorter form) originally appeared in *Etc. A Review of General Semantics* 9 (1951), pp. 3-8.

and beyond the operation of something as a sign within a sign process (or sign behavior). As such, it adds nothing to the account which has been given.

In *Signs, Language, and Behavior* four main uses of signs were discussed. They were then called the informative, valuative, incitive, and systemic uses of signs. Signs may be used to inform someone of the properties of objects or situations, or to induce in someone preferential behavior toward some objects or situations, or to incite a specific course of action, or to organize the dispositions to behavior produced by other signs. There is no necessary selection of such uses in terms of the kinds of signification which signs have. But, in general, designative signs are used informatively, appraisive signs are used valuatively, prescriptive signs are used incitively, and formative signs are used systemically.

The distinguishing feature of work in semiotic in recent years has been the extension of interest into the diversity of dimensions of signification and into the variety of uses which signs perform. Earlier in the century, philosophers were concerned mainly with the designative and formative dimensions of signification as they occurred in science and mathematics.[15] This concern remains, but it has been supplemented by a growing interest in the place that signs have in the manipulatory and consummatory phases of action. Thus attention has been increasingly directed to rituals, myths, morality, art, law, politics, religion, and philosophy. Since these topics involve values, I shall turn now to the theory of value (axiology), the relation of signs and values, and the place of values in human action.[16]

---

[15] Of course this was not true of thinkers such as Ernst Cassirer, who was concerned with all the major forms of human symbolic activity.

[16] Some readers may be interested in how the account of the present chapter differs from that of *Signs, Language, and Behavior*. There is here a different formulation of sign behavior, an attempt to do away with the formative dimension of signification, and in general a greater stress on the dimensions of signification (earlier called "modes of signifying").

2

Values, Signs, and the Act

§ 1. THE CONCEPT OF VALUE

The difficulties with the term 'meaning' in semiotic are paralleled by those with the term 'value' in axiology.[1] Both terms have such a variety of significations and uses that they serve only to indicate in a vague way an area of investigation, but do not advance its analysis. Just as we sought in Chapter 1 to identify a kind of behavior to ground the terms of semiotic, we now seek to identify a kind of behavior as a basis for introducing the terms of axiology.

Let us focus attention on "preferential behavior." An organism may be said to exhibit positive preferential behavior to an object or situation if it acts so as to maintain the presence of this object or situation, or to construct this object or situation if it is not present.[2] It exhibits negative preferential behavior if it seeks to move away from this object or situation, or to destroy or prevent

---

[1] For a discussion of the general relation of semiotic and axiology, see Edward Schouten Robinson, "The Languages of Sign Theory and Value Theory," in *The Language of Value*, R. Lepley, ed. (New York: Columbia University Press, 1957), pp. 29-57. See also my comments on this paper and Robinson's reply to these comments.

[2] Something like "preferential behavior" is common to such terms as 'selective-rejective behavior' (Dewey) and 'interest' (Perry). All such terms are vague, but in one way or another they require the behavior in question to cover a certain time span (see 'maintain' in the text). A single act of selection or favoring one thing over another is common to all behavior, and this is at best a single piece of evidence for preferential behavior.

the occurrence of this object or situation. Since the life process depends on the selection or rejection of certain objects or situations, preferential behavior (positive or negative) is a basic phenomenon of life. I have proposed that axiology (as the study of "value") be considered as the study of preferential behavior.[3]

Such behavior, as in the case of sign behavior, can be in principle studied scientifically ("objectively,"). But as in the case of sign behavior, in some cases it can be experienced, and reported upon, by the active agent himself. In the case of axiology, however, as in the case of semiotic, the scientific approach is in many cases more basic than the approach through self-observation and its reports, since animals and young persons are not able to report their "values," and older persons often report them vaguely or even erroneously. One student who said he disliked a certain painting very much was asked why. He said he did not like landscapes. But in the large set of paintings he had been shown, he had given very high preference ratings to a number of landscapes. So even if his statement about disliking the given painting was a correct report of his preferential behavior to it, his reasons given for such behavior were incorrect. It is to be expected that this is the case for much of human preferential behavior.

§ 2. VALUES AND PREFERENTIAL BEHAVIOR

It is customary, and important, to make a distinction between social and individual values. In the Constitution of the United States, a certain mode of social organization and procedure is favored, and the citizens of the United States, by and large, hold in common the disposition to behave in accordance with terms set out in the document. To the extent that they do so, they share a set of social values. Within such a large group there are smaller groups, such as members of a profession, of a religious organization, of a family, of a sports team, which have their own distinguishing set of social values. Moreover, there is the preferential behavior of single individuals toward specific persons, art objects,

---

[3] See Charles Morris, "Axiology as the Science of Preferential Behavior," in *Value: A Cooperative Inquiry*, R. Lepley, ed. (New York: Columbia University Press, 1949), pp. 211-222.

books, ideas, and ways to live, which may be called individual values. Both social and individual values involve preferential behavior and are in principle open to scientific investigation.

A "value situation" is regarded here as any situation in which preferential behavior occurs. Such behavior may be directed to any object or complex of objects, or to any properties of an object or complex of objects—hence to pains, joys, persons, actions, physical objects, signs, and complex structures of various sorts. A value situation, so conceived, is inherently relational, involving an action of (positive or negative) preferential behavior by some agent to something or other. Thus a pain as such would not be a "value," but it would be a negative value if responded to by negative preferential behavior, and a positive value if responded to by positive preferential behavior (which is at least sometimes the case).

So conceived, values are "objectively relative";[4] that is, they are properties of objects (in a wide sense of this term) relative to preferential behavior. They are properties of objects in the sense that edibility is a property of objects, but whereas edibility is a property of objects relative to digestive systems, values are properties of objects relative to preferential behavior.

Such a view avoids the ancient dispute among value theorists as to whether values are "subjective" or "objective"—for they are envisaged as properties of objects (or properties of properties of objects) relative to a "subject" (conceived of as responding by preferential behavior). Hence, they involve both subjects (agents) and objects. The relations of objects to agents (or "subjects") are no less "objective" than the relations of objects to other objects.

Not only is a value situation reportable in principle by others ("from without"), but it may also be experienced and reported upon by the agent who is himself in the situation. Here his language may be in such terms as 'I like (or dislike) X', 'I find X satisfying (or dissatisfying)', 'X is good (or bad)!'. The present hypothesis is that such expressions are reports by the agent upon the same value situation as are the reports of other persons upon this situation. Although the agent in a process of self-observation

---

[4] For objective relativity in general, see George H. Mead, "The Objective Reality of Perspectives," *The Philosophy of the Present*, A. Murphy, ed. (LaSalle, Ill.: Open Court Publishing Co., 1932), pp. 161-175.

has access to certain properties of the situation to which other observers do not have such direct access, it does not follow that it is not the same value situation being reported upon in both cases.[5]

§ 3. OPERATIVE, CONCEIVED, AND OBJECT VALUES

If we do not think of "values" in the abstract, but of value situations as considered here, then it becomes understandable why the term 'value' is so vague—in different contexts it is used to signify different aspects of value situations. Three of these usages are basic.

In the first place, the term 'operative value' signifies the direction of preferential behavior of a given individual in a variety of situations. If a person who is shown pairs of paintings, each pair consisting of a landscape and a portrait, always (or for the most part) chooses the portraits, we can say that his operative value is for portrayals of persons rather than landscapes. 'Operative value' in this sense is not limited to persons but holds wherever there is a direction of preference at choice points in behavior. A dog may positively value his master's beef as against canned dog food.

In the second place, positive or negative preferential behavior may be accorded to a signified object or situation. Here one may speak of "conceived values." Some object or situation is signified and liked or disliked as signified.[6] The object or situation need not be present and need not even exist. Utopias are conceived values in this sense, as is a way of life that one would like to live but does not. Conceived values involve signs, but operative values

---

[5] For the defense of a related position, see Herbert Feigl, "Mind-Body, Not a Pseudoproblem," *Dimensions of Mind*, S. Hook, ed. (New York: Collier Books, 1961), pp. 33-44.

[6] A number of writers in the theory of value limit, in effect, 'value' to what is here called "conceived value." This is true of Dewey and Kluckhohn. For Kluckhohn value is not just a preference but a preference felt or considered as justified; values are conceptions of the desirable. See Clyde Kluckhohn, "Value and Value-Orientations in the Theory of Action," *Toward a General Theory of Action*, T. Parsons and E. A. Shils, eds. (Cambridge, Mass.: Harvard University Press, 1951), pp. 388-433.

do not necessarily involve signs. A conceived value may be the source of an operative value—one may actually try to bring about the conceived utopia or try to change one's way of living in the direction of the way signified as desirable. In both cultures and individuals, however, there is always some divergence between conceived and operative values, and the degree of divergence may offer important material for the study of social and personality disorders.

In the third place, the term 'value' is commonly applied to objects. Here I shall speak of "object values." Some objects (or situations) are such that they support (or would support) positive preferential behavior to them by some organisms. Others are such that contact with them leads to (or would lead to) negative preferential behavior by some organisms. Thus, as I have already argued, object values are objectively relative; i.e., they are properties of an object considered in relation to its ability to reinforce preferential behavior directed toward it by some organisms.[7]

The terms 'operative value', 'conceived value', and 'object value' apply, in this formulation, to different aspects of value situations, that is, to situations involving preferential behavior. This is why axiology is conceived here as the study of such behavior.[8]

§ 4. THREE ASPECTS OF SYSTEMS

If we think of a system as an organization that tends to maintain itself through change, then a system may be said to have "boundaries." There are thus three possibilities of relation for a system with respect to other systems or objects. Most (or all) systems have all three of these relations to varying degrees.

The system may require for its maintenance an input of mate-

---

[7] See B. F. Skinner: "As to value, so far as I can see, a value is simply a way of describing what is either immediately or in the long run reinforcing to man." (In *Daedalus*, Summer 1961, p. 576. The volume title of this issue is *Evolution and Man's Progress*.) A number of psychologists have expressed a similar view. For the general problem of the ascription of value to objects, see Clarence I. Lewis, *An Analysis of Knowledge and Valuation* (LaSalle, Ill.: Open Court Publishing Co., 1946), Chap. 17, especially p. 511.

[8] See Charles Morris, *Varieties of Human Value* (Chicago: University of Chicago Press, 1956), p. 11.

rial from other systems or objects. Hence, its boundaries must be permeable. In this sense it can be said to be *receptive* to other systems or objects, or to be *dependent* upon them.

The system may need to act positively in a way that secures control of other systems or objects. Thus not only may an organism be receptive to and dependent upon edible objects (as are some plants) but it may have mechanisms for seeking out such objects and subjecting them to its maintenance (as do animals). In this sense it can be said to be *dominant* in relation to other systems or objects.

A system, however, to remain a system must be able to keep its boundaries sufficiently intact. It cannot be receptive to everything, and it cannot permit other systems to dominate it in a way that destroys its own system characteristics. In this sense a system can be said to have mechanisms of *detachment* to maintain its independence.

Systems can of course have subsystems as members, or be members of a supersystem. Thus human organisms have organs and cells as subsystems, and are in turn subsystems of social systems. The relations here are reciprocal. The functioning of the subsystem is dependent upon the functioning (or malfunctioning) of the supersystem, which is in turn dependent upon the functioning (or malfunctioning) of the subsystems.

§ 5. THE PRIMARY VALUES AND SIGNS

Dependence, dominance, and detachment, when so considered, are primary "dimensions" of value—operative values in action, object values of some phases of action, conceived values in various ethical, philosophical, and religious systems. They are primary in the sense that they correspond to, or are involved in, the three basic phases of action.

In the perceptual stage of the act, the detachment dimension of value is involved. The actor is seeking objects answering to his impulse—he is not yet committed to specific objects or ways of acting toward them. His boundary is being neither invaded nor extended over other things. He is in this sense detached. The signs appropriate to this stage of action are primarily designative. They serve to signify what sorts of things the actor will encounter.

In the manipulatory stage of the act, the dominance dimension of value is involved. The actor must now gain control of objects in his environment, securing them or constructing them as the case may be. In this sense he is extending his boundary to include other objects or systems. The signs corresponding to this phase of action are primarily prescriptive. They signify appropriate courses of action in the given situation.

In the consummatory stage of the act, the dependence dimension of value is involved. The actor must now let the selected and secured object work upon him. His boundaries must to this extent be permeable. To this extent he is dependent (or receptive). The signs at this stage are primarily appraisive. They signify the consummatory properties of objects in relation to his guiding impulses.

These relations are exhibited in Table 2. Such, I suggest, are the basic relations of signification and significance to each other and to action.

Table 2. *Stages of Action in Relation to Dimensions of Signifying and Value*

STAGES OF ACTION	DIMENSION OF SIGNIFYING	DIMENSION OF VALUE
Perceptual	Designative	Detachment
Manipulatory	Prescriptive	Dominance
Consummatory	Appraisive	Dependence

Actions, however, differ to the extent to which the three stages of action are predominant. There are persons whose main activity (at least professionally) remains primarily at the perceptual stage, whose signs are predominantly designative, and whose value is predominantly detachment. There are other persons whose main value is dominance and whose signs are primarily prescriptive. And finally there are persons who endeavor to live mainly at the stage of consummation—they are primarily dependent (or receptive), and the signs which they respond to or produce are strongly appraisive. These variations[9] reflect in part the differences be-

---

[9] See Lyle V. Jones and Charles Morris, "Relations of Temperament to the Choice of Values," *Journal of Abnormal and Social Psychology* 53 (1956), pp. 345-349.

tween the scientist, the technologist, and the artist.[10] Corresponding differences are exhibited in social institutions and in cultures.

§ 6. INDIVIDUAL AND SOCIAL FORMS OF THE PRIMARY VALUES

Each of the three primary dimensions of value has two manifestations, depending upon whether action is individual or social. "Social action" is action involving the mutual interaction of a number of individuals. Such action has the three stages already outlined. Thus a community that plans to build a bridge over a river must survey the possible sites of construction, must decide on methods of construction, and must aim at certain consummatory experiences rather than others (quickness of crossing, perhaps, as opposed to the view that crossing will reveal). Detachment, dominance, and dependence (or receptivity) are involved here as in the case of individual action, but different individuals may operate in the different phases of action. Thus the views and the work of scientists, technologists, and artists may all be considered in the planning and construction of the bridge.

Detachment, dominance, and dependence are somewhat different according to whether the individual or social action is the point of reference. Detachment may be detachment from a social group (as in certain early forms of Buddhism) or may be primarily restrained and self-controlled within a social group (as in some forms of Stoicism). Dominance for the individual may be the climbing of a mountain, or for a social group may be the control of its environment or other social groups. Dependence (or receptivity) for the individual may be enjoyment of his impulses in the immediate environment, while with respect to social action it may be dependence upon other persons in a social group.

In *Varieties of Human Value*, thirteen possible ways to live were rated by many subjects on a seven-point scale where 7 = like very much, 6 = like quite a lot, 5 = like slightly, 4 = indifferent, 3 = dislike slightly, 2 = dislike quite a lot, 1 = dislike very much. It was shown that these seven categories could be used statistically as

---

[10] Charles Morris, "Science, Art and Technology," *Kenyon Review* 1 (1939), pp. 409-423.

if they were integers, and that their use was similar across cultures (at least for the United States, Canada, Norway, China, India, and Japan).[11] This makes it possible, at least in this area, to compare conceived values quantitatively in a number of cultures. Table 3 lists the thirteen ways to live.

Table 3. Essential Emphases of the Ways to Live

Way 1: Preserve the best that man has attained
Way 2: Cultivate independence of persons and things
Way 3: Show sympathetic concern for others
Way 4: Experience festivity and solitude in alternation
Way 5: Act and enjoy life through group participation
Way 6: Constantly master changing conditions
Way 7: Integrate action, enjoyment, and contemplation
Way 8: Live with wholesome, carefree enjoyment
Way 9: Wait in quiet receptivity
Way 10: Control the self stoically
Way 11: Meditate on the inner life
Way 12: Chance adventuresome deeds
Way 13: Obey the cosmic purposes

More important in the present context is the fact that in the United States (and in the Indian) data five factors or dimensions were found among the thirteen ways to live.[12] These were identified as follows:

Factor A: Social Restraint and Self-Control. The stress here is upon responsible, conscientious, intelligent participation in human affairs. The orientation is primarily moral. There is awareness of the larger human and cosmic setting in which the individual lives and an acceptance of the restraints which responsibility to this larger whole requires. The accent is upon the appreciation and conservation of what man has attained rather than upon the initiation of change. The antithesis of this factor is unrestrained and socially irresponsible enjoyment.

Factor B: Enjoyment and Progress in Action. In this case, the stress is upon delight in vigorous action for the overcoming of

---

[11] Charles Morris and Lyle V. Jones, "Value Scales and Dimensions," *Journal of Abnormal and Social Psychology* 51 (1955), pp. 523-535.

[12] See preceding reference and Charles Morris, *Varieties of Human Value* (Chicago: University of Chicago Press, 1956), pp. 31-34.

obstacles. The emphasis is upon the initiation of change rather than upon the preservation of what has already been attained. The temper is one of confidence in man's powers rather than one of caution and restraint. The orientation is outward to society and to nature. The antithesis of the factor is a life focused upon the development of the inner self.

Factor C: Withdrawal and Self-Sufficiency. A rich inner life of heightened self-awareness is stressed here. The self rather than society is the focus of attention. The emphasis is not one of self-indulgence, however, but is rather upon the simplification and purification of the self in order to attain a high level of insight and awareness. Control over persons and things is repudiated, but not deep sympathy for all living things. The antithesis of the factor is mergence of the self with the social group for group achievement and enjoyment.

Factor D: Receptivity and Sympathetic Concern. The emphasis is upon receptivity to persons and to nature. The source of inspiration comes from outside the self, and the person lives and develops in devoted responsiveness to this source. This factor is not as sharply defined as are the other factors. But a stress upon responsive and devoted receptivity is clearly a mode of orientation different from that represented by any other factor.

Factor E: Self-Indulgence (or Sensuous Enjoyment). Here sensuous enjoyment is stressed, whether this enjoyment is found in the simple pleasures of life or in abandonment to the moment. The emphasis upon social restraint and self-control characteristic of Factor *A* is rejected. The antithesis of the factor is responsible submission of one's self to social and cosmic purposes.

In an analysis of these factors and the ways to live from which they are derived, Factors *A* and *C* can be regarded as the social and individual forms of detachment, and Factors *D* and *E* as the social and individual forms of dependence. Factor *B* does not in the United States or Indian data differentiate between individual dominance directed to social ends, but the distinction does appear in the analysis of the Chinese data. On common-sense grounds there is no doubt as to the distinction. Thus we may call social dominance B_1 and individual dominance B_2.

26   *Values, Signs, and the Act*

This model is represented in Figure 1. The capital letters are the value factors. For this model considerable empirical sup-

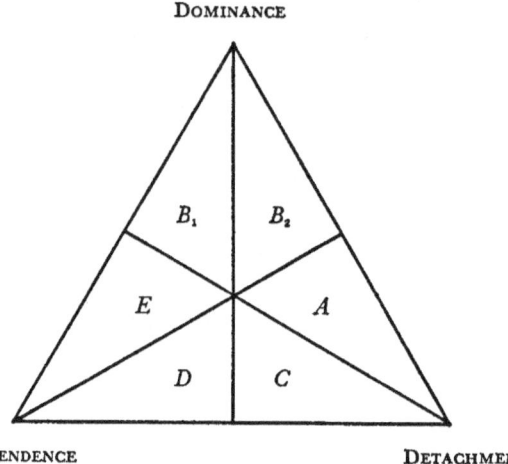

FIGURE 1. Model of the Relation of Values, Signs, and the Act.

B_1 and B_2: Dominance; manipulatory phase of the act; prescriptive dimension of signification.

A and C: Detachment; perceptual phase of the act; designative dimension of signification.

E and D: Dependence; consummatory phase of the act; appraisive dimension of signification.

port is available as to the three dimensions of value and their further distinction into individual and social forms. The relations of these value dimensions to the phases of action and to the dimensions of signification have less empirical support, though some relevant material points in this direction. In any case, the matter is open to empirical investigation.

§ 7. SIGNS, VALUES, AND INQUIRY

Signs and values, as discussed so far, can occur in behavior without there being any inquiry. Inquiry will be regarded here as a reflective process involving signs and directed to solving a problem.[13]

---

[13] Charles Morris, "Values, Problematic and Unproblematic, and Science," *Journal of Communication* 11 (1961), pp. 205-210. The present analysis is indebted to John Dewey, *Logic: The Theory of Inquiry* (New York: Henry Holt & Co., 1938).

Inquiry may be undertaken with regard to any of the phases of action. Problems may arise with respect to the perceptual, manipulatory, or consummatory phases of the act. Hence, there are three main types of problems to which inquiry is directed: (1) problems of what has happened, is happening, or will happen; (2) problems of what to do; (3) problems of what to accord preferential behavior. Inquiry will terminate in three different kinds of assertion with respect to these three different kinds of problems.

Inquiry into what has happened, is happening, or will happen terminates with designative statements and may be called *designative inquiry*. "The earth is five billion years old" is an instance of a designative statement. Empirical science may be regarded as one form of designative inquiry.

Inquiry into what to do terminates with prescriptive utterances and may be called *prescriptive inquiry*. "In case of disease X, operate in manner B rather than in manner A" is an instance of a prescriptive utterance. Technology, in a wide sense, represents a field of prescriptive inquiry.

Inquiry into what to prefer terminates with appraisive utterances and may be called *appraisive inquiry*. "Music A is better than music B" is an instance of an appraisive utterance. The field of criticism represents one form of appraisive inquiry.[14]

Thus one more column can be added to Table 2, to complete in Table 4 the representation of the basic model proposed in this study.

Table 4. Forms of Inquiry Related to Action, Signs, and Values

STAGES OF ACTION	DIMENSION OF SIGNIFYING	DIMENSION OF VALUE	FORMS OF INQUIRY
Perceptual	Designative	Detachment	Designative
Manipulatory	Prescriptive	Dominance	Prescriptive
Consummatory	Appraisive	Dependence	Appraisive

A problem arises only in a particular situation. Action encounters obstacles, and inquiry has as its aim the resolution of the problem so that action may proceed. In every problematic

---

[14] Mathematical inquiry is not analyzed in this account. It is presumably inquiry about, and in terms of, formative discourse. For some ideas on the possible relation of mathematics and logic, see Charles Morris, *Signs, Language, and Behavior* (New York: Prentice-Hall, 1946; New York: George Braziller, 1955), pp. 178-182.

situation there are features that are unproblematic.[15] The scientist never questions all at once the commonly accepted designative statements of his field; the technologist with a problem never questions all at once his accepted techniques; the critic always relies upon some unquestioned values in his critical activity. In all inquiry the problem is always surrounded by the area of the unproblematic, which gives the standards in terms of which the hypotheses arising in the inquiry are accepted or rejected.

In conducting any of these forms of inquiry, one uses the other forms of inquiry at various stages of the process. Thus the scientist, in moving toward designative statements, is constantly appraising one hypothesis as better than another and prescribing for himself various courses of experimentation. A similar situation exists for the technologist and critic. Thus the forms of inquiry are phases of, and emphases within, a more general process of inquiry.

§ 8. EVALUATIVE VERSUS NONEVALUATIVE INQUIRY

The distinction between appraisive and prescriptive inquiry is important. However, for certain purposes it is useful to lump them together as evaluative inquiry, in contrast to nonevaluative (or designative) inquiry. The main reason for this distinction is that the conclusions of evaluative inquiry (which are appraisals or prescriptions) always involve unproblematic values as *premises*, but while the conductor of designative inquiry (of which the scientist is a main example) always has unproblematic values, they do not act *as premises* in drawing his conclusions.

In trying to find out the age of the earth, the scientist will proceed according to the norms of scientific inquiry (such as taking account of all available evidence), and the main generalizations of earlier scientific inquiries will be accepted as unproblematic premises for drawing conclusions. The norms themselves

---

[15] The central idea of this paragraph is due to George H. Mead, "The Limits of the Problematic," Essay 2 in *The Philosophy of the Act*, pp. 26-44. See also Mead's essay "Scientific Method and Individual Thinker," *Creative Intelligence*, by John Dewey and others (New York: Henry Holt & Co., 1917), pp. 176-227.

will not, however, function as premises in the drawing of conclusions.

In evaluative inquiry one decides upon the course of preferential behavior—which objects are to be accorded preferential behavior and which course of action toward those objects is to be given preferential status. Knowledge is of course relevant to this process of evaluation, and the more scientific it is the better. One needs to know as fully and as accurately as possible the consequences of accepting one or another operative or conceived value. Therefore, as a phase of evaluation, one considers the consequences of various possible courses of preferential behavior. Evaluative inquiry, however, does more than this: it seeks for objects to which preference is to be given and for a course of action that will meet the value problems imposed by the inquiry.

§ 9. MEAD AND CERTAIN FEATURES OF HUMAN MENTALITY

It was characteristic of Mead to use interchangeably and without question what is variously called the alpha and omega points of view, the phenomenological and intersubjective points of view, the subjective and objective points of view, and others. I have tended in the past to label them the "self-inclusive" and "self-exclusive" points of view. All of these distinctions, in slightly different ways, mark the difference between the person as actor (including the activity of self-observation) and the person as observed by others than himself. We have met this distinction before and have suggested that these differences are due simply to points of system-reference—the same events or happenings being described from the focus of the actor or the focus of some other actor or actors. As Mead observed, an interpretation can be given behaviorally even of such terms as 'private' and 'subjective' without implying in any way the traditional mind-body dualism.[16]

Here, however, I wish to exploit Mead's insight in another

---

[16] See in *The Philosophy of the Act, op. cit.:* on privacy (as distinguished from the subjective), pp. 46-47, 376-385, 405; on mentality, pp. 70, 72; on consciousness, p. 73; on imagery, pp. 73, 377; on the relation of ideas, mind, and self to signs and symbols, pp. 189-190.

direction. For Mead it is characteristic of the human being that he can react to his own (or some of his) actions as other human beings will react. He tells a joke and laughs at it; he gives the clerk a ten-dollar bill and expects a certain amount of change in return; he phones his friend for an appointment and expects to meet him at a certain time and place.

Mead calls those symbols to which their producer is disposed to react like their receiver "significant symbols." He equates mind with the operation of such symbols. Mentality is thus for him a kind of behavior or disposition to behavior.

Mental processes become organized to varying degrees, and Mead often calls one form of this organization "reflective thought." All symbols involve conditioning; the symbols in reflective thought involve self-conditioning—man himself by the use of symbols is determining how he will react to certain other things. The man who decides to snub his friend has aroused in himself the disposition to react in a certain way when he meets the person in question. Mead used to say that John Watson conditioned his rats, but he did not explain how Watson himself was conditioned to do so.

Mead thought it was characteristic of man to modify his potential reactions in terms of the way other persons would react to them. Man, then, is always alternating between the self-inclusive and the self-exclusive points of view. He continually takes himself as an actor and as an object.

This capacity to respond by significant symbols is an intelligible basis for the analysis of the term 'freedom'[17] and for the conception of man as a moral agent.[18] Mead thus brings within his behavioral analysis what the traditional behaviorist ignores or denies or what the more complicated behaviorism of the present is still seeking after—a psychology adequate to the full human person.[19]

---

[17] Charles Morris, "The Mechanism of Freedom," *Freedom, Its Meaning*, R. N. Anshen, ed. (New York: Harcourt, Brace & Co., 1940).

[18] George H. Mead, "Scientific Method and the Moral Sciences," *International Journal of Ethics* 33 (1923), pp. 229-247.

[19] Contemporary psychology and philosophy at times begin to suggest positions integral to Mead's thought: The complementarity of the self-inclusive and self-exclusive points of view; the interpretation of privacy in terms of degree of accessibility to observation; the treatment of selves and societies as systems; a behavioral

I have introduced this account of one aspect of Mead's thought about man because of its relevancy to the topic of this chapter—values, signs, and the act. An analysis such as Mead's supports the objective relativity of values and clarifies the way in which the human being is able to engage in the type of inquiry earlier delineated—a type of inquiry which applies to value problems as well as to other problems and yet which gives grounds for certain distinctive features of evaluation.

Mead's analysis shows how the human being can take account of the values of others in his evaluations. It shows how the problematic (whether in evaluative or nonevaluative inquiry) is always surrounded by the unproblematic. Moreover, it shows how conceived values, operating through signs, can be effective in influencing through inquiry the course of individual and social behavior. Finally, it gives weight to the belief that a richly conceived behavioral approach can furnish a basis for the complex and subtle elaborations necessary in semiotic and axiology.

---

analysis of mind in terms of the significant symbol; the relation of thought to self-conditioning—these are among the many items that might be mentioned. The contemporary British, and to a certain extent American, philosophers seem to be drawing upon Mead without having read him. Mead, I believe, will come to be seen as the pivotal figure in the development of an adequate behavioral psychology and philosophy.

3

Semiotic and Some Issues in Contemporary Philosophy

§ 1. THE PHILOSOPHER'S CONCERN WITH LANGUAGE

A concern with the analysis of "meaning" is found in the writing of many contemporary philosophers. It has long been a focal point of discussion by the pragmatists and logical empiricists, and in recent decades it has become central in the work of the British analytical philosophers and those influenced by them.

A similar situation prevailed at the end of the Hellenistic period, during the late years of the Middle Ages, and during the Enlightenment[1] in the work of the French philosophers. Crises in culture led to crises in philosophy, and at such times the philosopher cannot simply take his philosophical language for granted but must make it an object of study to determine the nature and function of his work.

In modern philosophy the crisis was reflected, though in different ways, by Hume and by Kant. Owing to the influence of science, both philosophers were in a sense "empiricists." "Knowledge," even philosophical knowledge, applied only to what could

---

[1] See Charles Morris, "Semiotic and Scientific Empiricism," *Actes du Congrès International de Philosophie Scientifique—1935* (Paris: Hermann et Cie, 1936), Vol. 1, pp. 2-16. Reprinted in Charles Morris, *Logical Positivism, Pragmatism, and Scientific Empiricism* (Paris: Hermann et Cie, 1937), pp. 56-71.

be experienced, and the traditional notion that philosophy furnished a special knowledge, over and above science—a knowledge of "things in themselves," a kind of speculative cosmology—received a severe challenge. There are still many defenders of the traditional view, but more and more philosophers have felt the need for re-examining the nature of philosophic activity. There is at the present time no universally accepted view as to the nature of philosophy.

Hume and Kant both recognized that certain terms common in philosophy did not simply designate observable features of experience. Moral and religious and mathematical terms, for instance, were regarded as "meaningful," and these men each gave an analysis of such terms. But their analyses are not our present concern. What is relevant here is only that their influential positions resulted in an increasing concern by philosophers with the nature of langauge in general and the nature of philosophical language in particular. And attention could not be limited only to the signs that occur in natural science, but had to embrace moral, artistic, religious, mathematical, and philosophical signs. It is evident that a semiotic (or a number of semiotics) would have to be developed to deal with such problems.

Charles Peirce made an ambitious attempt to develop a semiotic. But since his views were influenced most by the way signs occur in science, mathematics, and formal logic, the dimensions of signification here called appraisive and prescriptive received no detailed or adequate treatment.

A similar and independent development took place in logical empiricism. A thinker such as Rudolf Carnap does not, to be sure, elaborate so comprehensive a framework for semiotic as Peirce did, but he has the same basic interest in the kind of "meaning" that scientific, mathematical, and logical signs have, and he does little with appraisals, prescriptions, or the process of evaluation.

In recent decades, however, these neglected aspects of sign processes have received an extensive consideration.[2] There are

---

[2] See, among many others: I. Hungerland, *Poetic Discourse*; Paul W. Taylor, *Normative Discourse*; Philip Wheelwright, *The Burning Fountain*; I. A. Richards, *Speculative Instruments*; T. A. Sebeok, ed., *Style in Language*; W. F. Zuurdeeg,

books on normative discourse, poetic discourse, religious discourse, and the like. And the philosophical journals are filled with articles analyzing terms such as 'good', 'right', 'ought', 'value', 'judgment of value'.

Most writers on these topics are handicapped by the lack of an elaborate enough semiotic and axiology to serve as instruments for their analyses. Many of the apparent conflicts seem to be due to different philosophers stressing various aspects of sign processes. In this chapter, I shall examine some current philosophical problems and positions in terms of the analysis given in Chapters 1 and 2. The treatment will be limited and schematic, and many important problems will not be dealt with. The aim is simply to suggest the philosophic relevance of the preceding analysis.

§ 2. AXIOLOGY AND "THE NATURALISTIC FALLACY"

That there are important differences between the "meanings" of such terms as 'pencil' and 'good' needs no argument. The problem is how to characterize the difference. G. E. Moore[3] early in the century pointed out that no set of "natural" properties could be substituted for 'good' in the utterance 'X is good', for then it is always possible to ask if having these properties is good. Thus if we propose that 'good' means "pleasure," we can then ask if pleasure *is* good; and since to say "pleasure is pleasure" is obviously not to say "pleasure is good," the proposed interpretation of the term 'good' is not tenable. Any attempt to give the "meaning" of 'good' by some set of natural properties was said to constitute "the naturalistic fallacy." Since 'good' was regarded as having *some* signification, it was claimed by Moore to signify a nonnatural property.

In terms of the present analysis the situation may be interpreted

---

An Analytical Philosophy of Religion; A. Cronbach, *The Realities of Religion*; L. B. Meyer, *Emotion and Meaning in Music*; K. E. Boulding, *The Image*; Ferruccio Rossi-Landi, *Significato, Comunicazione, e Parlare Comune*. An excellent bibliography is Ethel M. Albert and Clyde Kluckhohn, *A Selected Bibliography on Values, Ethics, and Esthetics* (Glencoe, Ill.: The Free Press, 1959).

[3] George E. Moore, *Principia Ethica* (Cambridge, England: Cambridge University Press, 1903).

as follows. Insofar as the term 'good' has an appraisive aspect, it does not designate any observable property of what is called good. A chemist's analysis of a food object does not find in the food an observable property of goodness in addition to whatever other properties his analysis reveals. If the properties his analysis reveals are called "natural properties," and then if 'good' signifies a property, it is of course possible to say (though this is a rather strange usage) that it signifies a nonnatural property. According to the present approach, on the contrary, it would simply be said that 'good', insofar as it is appraisive, does not designate but has appraisive signification.

But what is appraisive signification? The preceding analysis suggested that 'good' in its generic appraisive sense signifies the reinforcing properties of an object or situation, i.e., its capacity to support positive preferential behavior. Whether such a capacity is to be called "a property" depends upon how wide a signification the term 'property' is permitted to have. It is not a property independent of preferential behavior. But neither is the edibility of an object independent of a relation to some digestive system or other. Many persons (at least many philosophers) would not hesitate to say that edibility is a property of an object. Nor do I see any reason to deny that goodness is a property of an object; it is, if you will, a property of other properties, an "objectively relative" property. The distinction is marked by saying that 'good' in its appraisive signification does not designate, though it signifies an objectively relative property (the capacity to support positive preferential behavior) of something or other. To call such a property "nonnatural" seems ill-advised. It suggests philosophical problems that an analysis of the situation does not require. Being edible is, in common usage of the term 'natural', a natural property of certain objects relative to certain digestive systems, and in the same way there is no reason not to call "goodness" a natural property of certain objects or situations.

The follower of Moore will say, however, that to claim that 'good' signifies the property of supporting positive preferential behavior is still to commit the naturalistic fallacy in Moore's sense of the term. For if 'good', in some of its usages, signifies the capacity of an object to support positive preferential behavior, we can still ask whether this capacity is good—which indicates that we have not really stated the signification of 'good'.

The reply would be as follows. Even if the signification of 'good' is as stated, it is true that this does not give the full "meaning" of 'good', for the "meaning" of a term involves *both* its interpretant and its signification. Insofar as 'good' has appraisive meaning, it invokes in its interpreter a disposition to accord positive preferential behavior to what is otherwise signified. Now the phrase "capacity to support positive preferential behavior" need not have such an effect on its interpreter (i.e., need not have such an interpretant). Thus a biologist or psychologist may say that a certain object or situation has reinforcing properties for a certain animal. Here his signs may be entirely designative, referring to the observable relation between the object or situation and the behavior of the animal. His signs may not invoke in him or in any other interpreter a disposition to positive preferential behavior to the object or situation referred to. Hence, such signs are not appraisive signs since they do not have the interpretant that such signs require. Moore fails to distinguish the interpretant and the signification of normative signs.

§ 3. THE OUGHT AND THE IS

In Chapter 2, in the discussion of inquiry, it was admitted that a decision as to what ought to be done is never strictly deducible from statements as to what is or will be the case. But it was also maintained that there is no part of the domain of values upon which science is barred from having an influence. Since the problem of "the ought and the is" is a central issue in contemporary philosophy, the treatment of this issue in terms of the present approach requires elaboration.

The distinction between primarily appraisive and primarily prescriptive signs, as well as the related distinction between primarily appraisive and primarily prescriptive inquiry, suggests that the relation between 'good' and 'is' is not identical with the relation between 'ought' and 'is'. There are similarities, to be sure, and this is why a number of philosophers do not make much of the distinction, or they make the distinction within a common area of normative discourse or normative inquiry.

Norms or standards, as unproblematic values, are involved in both appraisive and prescriptive inquiry. Since behavior as well as other objects can be called "good," and since it is frequently claimed that certain objects or situations (other than acts) "ought to be," the line between the appraisive and the prescriptive is not easy to draw. The issue is further complicated by the fact that designative inquiry, as in natural science, is itself guided by norms or standards (such as what is to count as admissible evidence).

Nevertheless, it seems desirable to distinguish between inquiries into what is good and what ought to be done,[4] and to recognize a considerable independence of the two types of inquiry. There are many philosophers who hold that a determination of what is good involves the obligation that one ought to bring about that which is good. In a certain sense, this is undoubtedly the case; in general, appraisive signs accompany designative signs, and prescriptive signs accompany appraisive signs. Thus the religions, in prescribing how one should act, rest their case upon appraisals as to what is good, and these in turn are made in the light of statements as to the nature of man and the world.

Yet certainly the normative signification of something as good (as supporting positive preferential behavior) does not necessarily imply that one ought to act in a way to bring this object into existence or maintain its existence. Whether this is so or not will depend upon which unproblematic values are operative. A philosopher may claim that we should act so as to realize the good, and perhaps most philosophers do hold this view. But there have been philosophies (and religions) that have made the "ought" primary —the good is what we ought to bring about, and not simply what in fact is found desirable. Thus while judgments of obligation for the most part presuppose judgments of goodness, there is no purely theoretical reason why this should be the case. This is why in the present semiotical analysis the appraisive and the pre-

---

[4] See Clarence Irving Lewis, *The Ground and Nature of the Right* (New York: Columbia University Press, 1955).

scriptive are regarded as theoretically independent dimensions of signification. What relation they have for specific philosophies, or in specific situations, is then an empirical question.

Let us return to the problem of "the is and the ought." Admittedly, we cannot determine what ought to be done solely by determining what is the case, including the case of what now is being done. In this sense the "ought" is not deducible from the "is." There is nevertheless a dynamic interaction between prescriptions and designations. That adults should talk to children is a generally held human unproblematic value. If we were asked to support it by inquiry, we would of course point out that without such communication between the old and the young an infant organism would never become a human being, and no culture would perpetuate itself. Now these are "is" statements, but not statements of what is at the moment—rather they are statements of what will happen to certain dynamic processes if acted upon in certain ways. If we defend in inquiry that the old should talk to the young, we have, to be sure, the unproblematic values that children should become adult human beings and that cultures should continue. But we defend our position also in terms of what will in fact be the consequences of a course of action.

Thus the "is" and the "ought," while not identical and while not strictly deducible from each other, are in fact in dynamic interaction and mutually influence each other. The knowledge of what is and what will be under certain conditions is one factor in the control of conceived values as to what ought to be, and the acceptance of certain conceived values is one factor in the determination of what is and what will be. Such is the interaction of the "is" and the "ought"—and of designative and prescriptive inquiry.

§ 4. THE COGNITIVIST-EMOTIVIST CONTROVERSY

Much of recent philosophical controversy in the area of semiotic has been couched in terms of "cognitive meaning" versus "emotive meaning," or "referential meaning" versus "expressive meaning."

The pragmatists in general have argued that a normative term such as 'good' has a cognitive or referential meaning, and that judgments that something is good are controllable by empirical evidence. Some of the logical empiricists have taken the position that such a term as 'good' has no cognitive or referential meaning (and so cannot be controlled by empirical evidence) but simply expresses the "emotions" or "attitudes" of the producer of such a term.

Since none of these terms has been taken as basic in the present approach, certain problems of translation are involved. Let us take 'cognitive' and 'referential' as synonymous with 'having signification'.[5] In this framework, normative terms such as 'good' and 'ought' have a signification, a "reference" to reinforcing properties of objects or situations in the case of the appraisive dimension of signification, and to the instrumental properties of acts in the case of prescriptive signs.[6] If 'designation' is restricted to the signification of observable characteristics of objects or situations, such normative terms do not designate though they still have signification. They are subject to empirical control, but the evidence for their applicability differs from that of primarily designative signs: in the case of primarily appraisive signs the evidence for their interpreter concerns whether the object or situation does in fact support positive preferential behavior; in the case of primarily prescriptive signs the evidence for their interpreter concerns whether the prescribed act is in fact instrumental in the situation in which the prescription is made. This analysis supports the pragmatists' position that normative signs have a "cognitive" or "referential" aspect; i.e., they have a kind of signification. At the same time this analysis admits with the "emotivist" (or "noncognitivist") that normative terms cannot be characterized solely in terms of their signification. Such terms have distinctive kinds of interpretants. The "meaning" of terms involves both their significations and their interpretants. The

---

[5] The term 'cognitive', in contrast to 'noncognitive', is a very ambiguous word. Frankena distinguishes nine possible meanings of 'cognitive'. See W. K. Frankena, " 'Cognitive' and 'Non-Cognitive,' " in *Language, Thought, and Culture*, P. Henle, ed. (Ann Arbor, Mich.: University of Michigan Press, 1958), pp. 146-172.

[6] For an experimental analysis of the signification of 'good' and 'ought', see Charles Morris, *Varieties of Human Value* (Chicago: University of Chicago Press, 1956), pp. 164-168, 170-176.

interpretant of such normative terms seems to be what the "emotivist" is signifying by the terms 'attitude' or 'emotion'. Further, since we have seen that in one usage of 'express' a sign may be said to express (but not signify) its interpretant, the present approach can account for the emotivists' claim that normative terms are "expressive." The analysis then may claim to have done justice to the position of both the pragmatists and the emotivists. Each group has stressed certain aspects of sign processes that a more comprehensive semiotic can admit.

There are a number of analyses by contemporary philosophers which in their own way move in the direction of the present approach. Let us take Philip Blair Rice as an example.[7]

In his book *On the Knowledge of Good and Evil*, Rice says of normative terms and judgments:

> We have treated such terms and judgments as having both a prescriptive and a descriptive component, as making at the same time a knowledge claim and an incitement to an action or an attitude. It makes little difference whether we say, in general, that a normative judgment is a cognitive statement with a prescriptive function or that it is a prescriptive expression whose meaning includes a cognitive assertion resting on empirical evidence. All that matters is to include both elements.[8]

Thus for him a normative term is "dual in nature, consisting of a Matrix Meaning which is non-cognitive in its force, and an Identifying Property which is a natural property."[9] His "Matrix Meaning" corresponds to our "interpretant," and his "Identifying Property" to our "signification." The "meaning" of a normative term, in his account and ours, involves both aspects.[10]

---

[7] Philip Blair Rice, *On the Knowledge of Good and Evil* (New York: Random House, 1955).

[8] *Ibid.*, pp. 271-272.

[9] *Ibid.*, p. 119.

[10] Rice also holds a position similar to the value unproblematic analysis given in Chapter 2 of the present account (*ibid.*, p. 111), and he recognizes that normative conclusions involve normative premisses. He does not distinguish 'good' and 'ought' as does the present account. 'Good' expresses for him a conditional prescription and 'ought' an unconditional one (*ibid.*, p. 197). Charles L. Stevenson also recognizes that normative terms have both a "referential" and an "emotive" aspect, maintaining that the "emotive" aspect gives them their distinctive character. Stevenson also has consistently identified meaning with a disposition to respond

§ 5. THE ABSOLUTIST-RELATIVIST CONTROVERSY

No controversy is more persistent among philosophers than the controversy as to whether "judgments of value" (appraisive evaluations) and "judgments of obligation" (prescriptive evaluations) are "absolute" or "relative." A more misleading formulation is whether such judgments are "objective" or "subjective." How does this controversy appear in the framework of the present approach? In Chapter 2, a defense was made of the "objectively relative" nature of judgments of value and of obligation. Here the analysis will be applied to one specific problem.

In the study of thirteen possible ways to live it was found that they combined in various ways different emphases upon dependence, dominance, and detachment, each in turn having a predominantly egocentric or social orientation. The problem may then be raised as to which of the thirteen ways to live (or which combination of the value dimensions) is "the best." The related question concerns the way one "ought" to live. The absolutist (or objectivist) would believe that these questions could be given definitive answers. The relativist would believe that no such definitive answers could be given. The objective relativist would maintain that objective answers could be given but only in relation to specific contexts with their own unproblematic values.

Can detachment, dominance, and dependence be given an absolute ordering in terms of values? The absolutist would say yes, and in various cultures at various times this has been done. The West, in some of its more characteristic manifestations, has put them in this order: dominance, dependence, detachment. Some forms of ancient Eastern culture have favored another order: detachment, dependence, dominance. It is clear, however, that the contemporary Orient is changing this ordering in favor of dominance and that the priority of dominance as a value is beginning to be questioned by a number (as yet small) of Westerners.

From the point of view of objective relativism, these changes are related to what is happening in the different cultures. With the development of modern technology, the Oriental nations now

---

in regular fashion to "words." See his *Ethics and Language* (New Haven, Conn.: Yale University Press, 1944).

have the possibility of controlling their environment toward the reduction of poverty, hunger, and disease—thus the stress on dominance is now more appropriate. Western nations have secured considerable control of their environment (at least their physical environment), and the consequences of the extreme emphasis on power have been made visible in the world wars—thus more Westerners than previously have begun to question power as the supreme value.

In the case of an individual, a subject who had previously shown a strong preference for ways of life stressing activity, adventure, and power at a later time favored ways to live that made meditation and detachment central. An investigation showed that in the interval he had developed a serious and perhaps permanent heart injury. His earlier and later judgments of value and obligation might be considered as objectively correct relative to his earlier and later physical conditions.

It might be claimed that the preceding analysis of the nature of action permits a more positive answer to the questions raised. For if perception, manipulation, and consummation are the basic aspects of action, then it might be claimed that the best way to live, and the way one ought to live, would be a life combining the values of detachment, dominance, and dependence. In the abstract perhaps this claim may be admitted—as an objective value judgment relative to the most general features of human action. But even here the way in which these values are to be weighted will depend in concrete cases upon the differences between individuals, the differences among institutions in a specific culture, and the problems that specific cultures confront at a given moment in their historical development.

Paul Taylor, in *Normative Discourse*,[11] defends the position that there is *a* best way to live and that this way can in principle become an object of rational choice. He is concerned with defending "absolutism" on this issue, as opposed to "scepticism" and "relativism." However, one of the requirements of a rational choice between ways to live in his analysis is that one should not be committed to a way of life. This would mean, in the present

---

[11] Paul Taylor, *Normative Discourse* (Englewood Cliffs, N.J.: Prentice-Hall, 1961).

terms, that no unproblematic values concerning ways to live were in fact serving as the basis of the choice; and according to the present proposed objective relativism (applied to appraisive and prescriptive inquiry), this seems never to be the case. The stress on context in such inquiry is in opposition to Taylor's defense of "absolutism."

While Taylor holds that there is *one* best way to live, rationally determinable, he admits this is an ideal—"no one knows, or will know, what that way of life is." Hence, he writes that we need to have an "open" society "which tolerates and even encourages great diversity in ways of life and the freedom to choose among them."[12] This was the conclusion of my book *The Open Self*. While I claimed that there is some general historical tendency to favor a life including all the values of dependence, dominance, and detachment, any particular way to live combines them in various ways, and the choice between these particular ways to live is an objectively relative choice, always made in a context, and is neither purely "relative" nor even ideally "absolute."

§ 6. SEMIOTIC, AXIOLOGY, AND PHILOSOPHY

It was stated earlier that there is at present no universal agreement as to the meaning of the term 'philosophy'. There are currently many possible explications of the term.

I have indicated one possible view of the relation of semiotic and axiology, conceived as the studies of sign behavior and preferential behavior. They are overlapping disciplines. While signs generally occur in behavior in which operative and conceived values are involved, there are aspects of sign behavior that may be studied without reference to values, and there are aspects of preferential behavior whose study involves no reference to signs. The overlap of the two disciplines comes in the study of predominantly appraisive and prescriptive signs, for such study is equally a part of semiotic and of axiology.

How may one conceive the relation of philosophy to axiology, to semiotic, and to their overlap? There are many possible answers

---

[12] *Ibid.*, pp. 331-332.

44   *Semiotic and Contemporary Philosophy*

to this question. Insofar as philosophers analyze judgments of value and obligation, they are working within the overlap of axiology and semiotic, and their work not only depends on the existing development of such disciplines but also makes contributions to them. The preceding discussions in this chapter bear witness to this reciprocal relation.

This relation by itself, however, does not delimit the work of the philosopher, nor in the present context is such an attempt at delineation suggested.[13] There are those today who think of philosophy as essentially logic, as the philosophy of science, as speculative cosmology, as an inquiry into the nature of man, as evaluation with respect to man's most general value problems. These are all respectable inquiries, regardless of what name is applied to them. Their diversity attests the contemporary uncertainty as to what philosophy is about, but it also attests the range and vigor of contemporary philosophers. In some usages the term 'philosophy' is limited to general designative inquiry, in others appraisive inquiry is permitted, in others prescriptive inquiry is the focus, in still others philosophy is thought of as the proposal of the most general linguistic frameworks.

The only point to be made here is that these different conceptions of philosophy can be stated in semiotical and axiological terms, and that philosophic inquiry is in turn one source (though not the only source) of semiotical and axiological clarification and progress.

Semiotic and axiology are emerging as scientific disciplines. Their relation to philosophical analysis and synthesis will in time be no different from the relation of philosophy to other scientific disciplines—however that relation is conceived.

§ 7. PHILOSOPHY AND PRAGMATICS

Pragmatics is the aspect of semiotic concerned with the origin, uses, and effects of signs. The pragmatists, as philosophers, have

---

[13] I suggested two different explications of the term 'philosophy' in the closing paragraph of *Foundations of the Theory of Signs* (Chicago: University of Chicago Press, 1938) and in *Signs, Language, and Behavior* (New York: Prentice-Hall, 1946), pp. 233-238. But there are many more possibilities. It now seems to me questionable to speak of *the* meaning of the term 'philosophy'.

stressed the problems in this area, and it was for this reason that 'pragmatics' was introduced into the terminology of the present semiotic. In the early stages of logical empiricism, the field of pragmatics was acknowledged but was regarded as an empirical discipline and not properly philosophical. Recently several developments have occurred.

One is the recognition that to talk of the origin, uses, and effects of signs requires the devolopment of a language in which to do such talking. This means that a distinction must be made between "pure" (or logical or formal) pragmatics and "descriptive" (or empirical) pragmatics, analogous to the distinction between pure and descriptive semantics and between pure and descriptive syntactics. Carnap has moved in this direction, and Richard Martin is intensively exploring this area.[14] It becomes possible to think of logic as the pure (or formal or analytic) portion of semiotic, with a pure pragmatic as well as a pure semantic and pure syntactic domain.

The British analysts of the "ordinary language" emphasis have also been stressing the pragmatics of signs (especially normative signs). They wish to deal only with the "logical" aspects of signs in order to distinguish their work from that of the linguists. But the term 'logical' is by no means clear in their usages. They do not in general attempt to formulate a developed semiotic, and they are apparently caught in the dilemma of trying to deal with the pragmatics of ordinary language in a way that is in one sense empirical and in another sense not empirical but "logical." In any case, the work of the British analysts furnishes another instance of the concern of contemporary philosophy with pragmatics. It seems possible that the solution of such problems as the British analysts face might be helped by an explicit semiotic.

Another place where pragmatics is relevant to contemporary philosophy is in its growing concern with the choice of "conceptual frameworks" in the sciences and in philosophy. It is now widely admitted that the acceptance or rejection of such lin-

---

[14] Rudolf Carnap, "On Some Concepts of Pragmatics," *Philosophical Studies* 6 (1955), pp. 89-91. Reprinted in the enlarged edition of *Meaning and Necessity* (Chicago: University of Chicago Press, 1956), pp. 248-250; Richard M. Martin, *Toward a Systematic Pragmatics* (Amsterdam: North-Holland Publishing Co., 1959), and *Intension and Decision* (Englewood Cliffs, N.J.: Prentice-Hall, 1963).

guistic frameworks involves pragmatical considerations[15] (simplicity, fruitfulness in carrying out inquiry, accordance with the ideology of the time or of a given thinker, and the like). Thus the investigation of the acceptance and transformation of linguistic frameworks (scientific and philosophical) is a semiotical investigation that involves the area of pragmatics.[16]

Another central issue in contemporary philosophy is whether a sharp distinction can be made between analytic and synthetic sentences (or "propositions"). In the present context this is the question of whether a sharp distinction can be made between formative and lexical discourse. I have suggested elsewhere that the distinction can be made only in terms of pragmatic considerations —and not in terms of semantics or syntactics alone. This seems to be implicitly involved in Carnap's introduction of "meaning postulates"[17] in his defense of the distinction of the analytic and the synthetic. To decide whether the sentence "All crows are black" is analytic or synthetic involves reference to the sign structure (and hence to the dispositions to respond) of a specific interpreter (or a group of interpreters). If the interpreter is disposed at a certain time to respond to all denotata of the term 'crow' by the term 'black' (i.e., if he would not call anything a crow unless it were black), then the sentence is analytic at that time; otherwise it is not. The criterion is thus pragmatic and involves the use of signs (i.e., the acceptance of a sign framework)

---

[15] See Rudolf Carnap, "Empiricism, Semantics, and Ontology," *Revue Internationale de Philosophie* 11 (1950), pp. 208-228. Reprinted in Carnap's *Meaning and Necessity* (Chicago: University of Chicago Press, enlarged edition, 1956), pp. 205-221. See the concluding paragraph for the view that "the acceptance or rejection of abstract linguistic forms, just as the acceptance or rejection of any other linguistic forms in any branch of science, will finally be decided by their efficiency as instruments, the ratio of the results achieved to the amount and complexity of the efforts required." For a similar statement, see W. V. O. Quine, *Word and Object* (Cambridge, Mass., The Technology Press of the Massachusetts Institute of Technology; New York: John Wiley & Sons, 1960), p. 274.

[16] See also Thomas S. Kuhn, "The Structure of Scientific Revolutions," in *International Encyclopedia of Unified Science*, Vol. 2, No. 2 (Chicago: University of Chicago Press, 1962); Philipp Frank, ed., *The Validation of Scientific Theories* (Boston: The Beacon Press, 1954).

[17] Rudolf Carnap, "Meaning Postulates," *Philosophical Studies* 3 (1952), pp. 65-73. Reprinted in his enlarged edition of *Meaning and Necessity* (Chicago: University of Chicago Press, 1956), pp. 222-229.

by a specific producer of the signs. 'Acceptance' is a basic term in pragmatics.

§ 8. CONCLUDING WORDS

A final word will clarify what has been done and what has not been done in this chapter. No attempt has been made to define philosophy or to deal in any thoroughgoing way with some of the problems that concern those contemporary philosophers whose orientation is to a large degree linguistic.

It cannot be said that contemporary philosophy gives complete support to the framework and results of analysis of this book. There are dissenters at every point. Nevertheless, on the basis of a much wider survey than the literature cited, some general directions are apparent:

1. The distinction between the semantic, syntactic, and pragmatic aspects of semiotic is widespread.

2. There are many philosophers who link the term 'good' with something like "supports positive preferential behavior."

3. There are many philosophic thinkers who admit the multidimensionality of such normative terms as 'good' and 'ought', i.e., who admit semantic, syntactic, and pragmatic dimensions to these terms in various circumstances.

4. There is considerable support for the view that 'good' and 'ought' differ basically as normative terms. This distinction is sometimes not made, though it is seldom deliberately challenged.

5. Many philosophers, though not all, admit something akin to "objective-relativism" in their discussion of normative terms. To this degree the older and simpler dichotomy of "subjective" and "objective" is seldom held today. The same is true for the dichotomy of "absolute" and "relative," and for the simple opposition of "emotive and referential meaning."

6. The discussion of "use" and "usage" has become very common in contemporary analyses, though these terms often have very different significations and are often confused with signification itself.

7. Pragmatics, as a part of semiotic, both in its descriptive and pure forms, plays an increasingly great part in contemporary philosophical discussions of signs.

8. There is wide recognition that it is necessary to consider language in all its multiplicity of significations and uses.[18]

Apparently the term 'meaning' still bedevils many philosophic discussions in this area by being introduced or dismissed too summarily. The crucial distinction of interpretant and signification is rarely made and is the source of much confusion. The various dimensions of signification are seldom clearly distinguished. The analyses in general are not grounded in a way that at least allows the possibility of empirical control—as a behavioral analysis does, or the analyses of the professional linguist. It is thus difficult to decide between the claims of divergent analyses and, indeed, to know whether what is being claimed is regarded as an empirical statement or as a proposal of a way to employ certain terms.

---

[18] While this is a view of many philosophers, it is seldom carried out in detail. The linguists have done much here. A valuable analysis is in the paper by Roman Jakobson, "Linguistics and Poetics," in *Style in Language*, Thomas Sebeok, ed. (Cambridge, Mass.: The Technology Press of Massachusetts Institute of Technology; New York: John Wiley & Sons, 1960), pp. 350-377. He distinguishes six factors in any act of verbal communication, each of which determines a different function of language.

4

Semiotic, Axiology, and the Behavioral Sciences

§ 1. THE PROBLEM

The preceding chapters have presented in summary form the framework of a language for discussing signs, values, and their interrelations. As a general proposal of a linguistic framework to deal with material from many fields of study, the analysis is, in one sense of the term, philosophical. But since it is oriented around the concept of action, it is at least partly open to empirical controls. In this chapter I shall consider some of the theoretical and empirical work in the behavioral sciences that is relevant to the model proposed here. I shall begin with psychology.

§ 2. THE NATURE OF THE INTERPRETANT

The interpretant of a sign has been characterized as a disposition, caused by the sign, to respond in a certain kind of way. The interpreter of the sign can under certain conditions report by self-observation what he observes when something is operating for him as a sign.[1] But if, as in the present approach, such reports are regarded as reports on only certain aspects of action processes, they cannot furnish a full account of the interpretant.

---

[1] See Eugene T. Gendlin, *Experiencing and the Creation of Meaning* (New York: The Free Press of Glencoe, 1962).

Those psychologists who reject, or regard as inadequate, the self-observational approach, may proceed in either of two ways. On the one hand, they may interpret the disposition to respond set up by a sign as being simply the probability that a certain kind of response will occur under certain conditions. On the other hand, they may regard the interpretant as some sort of mediational process occurring in the organism,[2] aroused by some stimulus which in turn provides the stimuli for some other, ultimately overt, act. Such mediational views are very common among behavioral psychologists.[3] Here I shall be concerned, however, with the views of Charles E. Osgood for two reasons: he regards his work as an attempt to clarify the notion of "disposition" as has been used here, and his studies are a sustained attempt to control his notion of a "representational-mediational process" by experimental investigations.[4]

Osgood's basic model is as follows. An animal, say a rat, is given an electrical shock and responds to it in observable ways. Now if another stimulus, say the sound of a buzzer, is presented slightly before the shock, it may itself come to evoke *some part* of the same reaction elicited by the shock. This partial reaction will in turn produce stimuli which may in turn be linked with overt responses which are instrumental in getting away from or perhaps avoiding the shock—thus the rat may learn when the buzzer

---

[2] For earlier forms of this position, see Albert E. Goss, "Early Behaviorism and Verbal Mediating Responses," *American Psychologist* 16 (1961), pp. 285-298.

[3] See, for example: John P. Seward, "The Sign of a Symbol: A Reply to Professor Allport," *Psychological Review* 55 (1948), pp. 277-296; O. Hobart Mowrer, *Learning Theory and the Symbolic Process* (New York: John Wiley & Sons, 1960); Clark L. Hull, *A Behavior System* (New Haven: Yale University Press, 1952).

[4] Charles E. Osgood, George J. Suci, and Percy H. Tannenbaum, *The Measurement of Meaning* (Urbana, Ill.: University of Illinois Press, 1957). Osgood's basic notion of a representational-mediational process has much in common with Clark Hull's "fractional antedating goal reaction." Roger Brown discusses Osgood's mediating process, and he believes there is no conclusive evidence for it. Here he tends to discount the whole mediation scheme. See his *Words and Things* (Glencoe, Ill.: The Free Press, 1958), pp. 101 ff. Yet in a paper written with Don E. Dulaney he said that if meaning is a response, "it must be, as Osgood suggests, a mediating implicit response." See "A Stimulus-Response Analysis of Language and Meaning," in *Language, Thought, and Culture*, Paul Henle, ed. (Ann Arbor, Michigan: University of Michigan Press, 1958), p. 84.

The Nature of the Interpretant 51

sounds to turn a wheel which prevents the shock. Osgood diagrams this as follows:

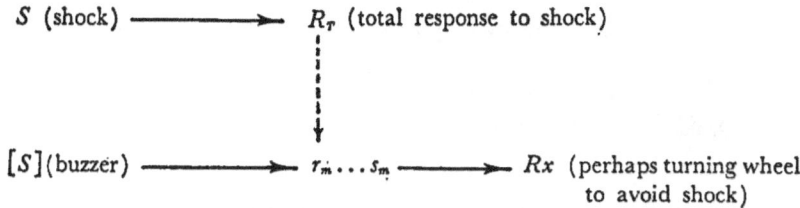

Here "$r_m \cdots s_m$" is the representational-mediational process. His "r_m" "represents" the shock since it is part of the reaction R_T to S (the shock), and it is "mediational" since it can be cued to behavior that avoids the shock. Osgood (as a psychologist) calls r_m the "meaning" of $[S]$ (the buzzer). Osgood claims the advantage of his formulation to be that it makes the whole of learning theory applicable to the study of signs.

The instrument that he has employed for such a study he calls the "semantic differential." In its common form a semantic differential consists of a set of bipolar scales called "good-bad," "warm-cool," "strong-weak," "angular-rounded," and the like. These are presented to subjects on scales with seven intervals, such as:

angular ____ ____ ____ ____ ____ ____ ____ rounded

The subject is then asked to check the place on the various scales of some other term (Osgood says "concept"). Thus 'angel' may be judged as very "good," "warm," and "rounded," while 'devil' may be judged as very "bad," "strong," and "angular." Osgood shows that the seven interval markings may be treated as numerical expressions, and that a numerical measure (called "distance") may be computed for the degree of similarity or dissimilarity between terms ("concepts" or "signs"). Osgood calls what is so measured the "connotative" (or, at times, the "metaphorical") meaning of the terms being judged on the semantic differential. He believes his technique does not isolate the "denotative meanings" of the terms being judged, since 'mother' and 'angel' may be very similar (have small "distance") on this test and yet clearly "denote" different kinds of objects. In our terms, the semantic differential is related to the interpretants of signs and some interrelations of their significations rather than their significations as such. Semiotically, Osgood's "connotative meaning" is very vague.

§ 3. DIMENSIONALITY AND THE SEMANTIC DIFFERENTIAL

An important further step taken by Osgood and his collaborators was the study of dimensions of "connotative meanings" in terms of the scales used in various forms of the semantic differential. The question is whether the terms ("concepts" or "signs") analyzed on these scales fall into a number of groups which have some "connotative meaning" in common. Using the technique of factor analysis, Osgood shows that this is in fact the case. This is the most important step yet taken toward an experimental and quantitative analysis of some aspects of the "meaning" of signs.

Osgood found that the terms 'good', 'true', and 'beautiful' clustered together; that is, if a term ("concept") was rated highly as good on the good-bad scale, it tended to be rated highly as true on the true-false scale and to be rated highly as beautiful on the beautiful-ugly scale. Osgood called this the *evaluative factor*. The other main factors (or dimensions) isolated by factor analysis were as follows: a *potency factor* for terms high in the "strong," "hard," "masculine" scales; an *activity factor* for terms high in the "active," "fast," "excitable" scales; a *stability factor* for terms high in the "stable," "predictable," "wise" scales; a *receptivity factor* for terms high in the "savory," "warm," "colorful" scales.

Each term analyzed on the basis of the semantic differential is given (by factor analysis) a numerical weight on each of the factors or dimensions. Thus we are told in quantitative terms to what degree a term is evaluative, potent, active, stable, and receptive.

Of interest here is the possible relation of such results to what I have called the three dimensions of signification, the three kinds of interpretants, and the three basic dimensions of value. No conclusive statements can be made, but some comments are necessary to illustrate the problems of subjecting the model I have proposed to experimental control.

In the first place, there is no necessary parallel between the semiotical dimensions of designation, appraisal, and prescription and the dimensions revealed in the Osgood studies. For the terms 'designation', 'appraisal', and 'prescription' are metalinguistic and are part of a proposed terminology for talking about signs, while the Osgood dimensions reveal relations between signs in the natural language. Nevertheless, some comparison of the relations between the two sets of dimensions is possible.

One of my students, Mr. James Alsobrook, used 67 bipolar scales, most of them from Osgood's studies; the others were scales (such as *required–not allowed*) added to get the prescriptive element not noticeable in the Osgood scales. Twenty-four students (eight graduates and sixteen undergraduates) were instructed in the use of the terms 'designative', 'appraisive', and 'prescriptive' and were then asked to rate the 67 scales in terms of how much each was designative, appraisive, and prescriptive. There was an agreement of 79 per cent as to whether a scale was predominantly designative, appraisive, or prescriptive. In a smaller group of eight graduates and eight undergraduates, the figure on the same task was 85 per cent, and there was 69 per cent agreement as to the relative strength of designation, appraisal, and prescription in the scales.

Since many Osgood scales were used in the Alsobrook study, it was possible to get a crude comparison between Osgood's main factors and the three categories of designative, appraisive, and prescriptive. The results for eight graduate students in a seminar on the theory of signs were as shown in Table 5.

Table 5. Designative, **Appraisive,** and Prescriptive Analysis of **Osgood Factors**

NUMBER OF SCALES USED	OSGOOD FACTOR	SCALE JUDGED AS PRIMARILY		
		DESIGNATIVE	APPRAISIVE	PRESCRIPTIVE
14	Evaluative	21%	79%	0%
11	Potency	100%	0%	0%
6	Activity	100%	0%	0%
2	Stability	50%	50%	0%
6	Receptivity	33%	67%	0%
7	Unassigned scales	100%	0%	0%

Thus while Osgood's evaluative and receptivity factors were regarded by these students as being primarily appraisive, his potency and activity factors were regarded as primarily designative. No one of the Osgood scales used was regarded as primarily prescriptive. The "unassigned scales" were those used by Osgood which had no numerical weight high enough to assign them to one of the Osgood factors. They are all regarded by the student judges as primarily designative. Thus in spite of Osgood's disavowals, the semantic differential does seem to distinguish in some degree between what Osgood calls "denotative meanings" and "connotative meanings," even if it cannot specify the difference in "denotative meaning" of two signs that have the same "connotative meaning." Osgood's work lends experimental support to the position that the domain of signification is multi-dimensional, but the interpretation of what these dimensions are is still unclear.

§ 4. OSGOOD'S FACTORS AND THE KINDS OF INTERPRETANTS

Osgood suggests that the "meaning" factors isolated by the semantic differential reflect differences in the representational-mediational sign behavior ($r_m \ldots s_m$). Since this multidimensionality of the interpretant is the position taken in the construction of the present model, there is general agreement in this respect with the view of Osgood. Daniel Berlyne noticed the possibility of comparing the two approaches. He suggested that the distinctions between predominantly appraisive, prescriptive, and designative signs could be translated into Osgood's scheme

> . . . by categorizing symbols according to which fractional component of the response pattern has come to form the r_m. If the r_m is composed mainly of emotional and drive-producing responses, it [the sign] is an appraisor, whereas if it consists largely of fractional skeletal responses, it is a prescriptor. Designators will thus be those symbols which are built up of responses dependent on the stimulus properties of the signification, and these may consist of perceptual responses or verbal responses of the kind Skinner calls "tacts."[5]

---

[5] Daniel Berlyne, "Knowledge and Stimulus-Response Psychology," *Psychological Review* 61 (1954), p. 248.

Thus Berlyne makes a place in Osgood's approach for an interpretant corresponding to designative signification, which is in harmony with the present approach. John B. Carroll, in a review of *The Measurement of Meaning*,[6] similarly suggests a "denotative" aspect for Osgood's evaluative, activity, and potency factors. He links "evaluative" with perceiving the object to be favorable or unfavorable, "activity" with how quick the activity must be with respect to the object, "potency" with how much strength would be needed to deal with the object. Similar analyses could no doubt be given for the "receptivity" and "stability" factors.

Arthur W. Staats[7] has experimentally shown that an independent "denotative" (or "designative") dimension can be isolated on such a semantic differential scale as "sharp-round." He was able to obtain significant differences on the scale by conditioning terms for sharp or round objects (which had about equal weights on the activity, potency, and evaluative factors) to nonsense syllables. The weights of the terms on these factors were about the same before and after the experiment, while the two nonsense syllables were given high weights on the "sharp" or the "round" end of the "sharp-round" scale.

These suggestions and studies, together with the materials presented in § 3 of this chapter, indicate that the semantic differential in its present form (and the "meaning" factors isolated by its use) does have a designative aspect. Nevertheless, it is clear that the instrument, as Osgood admits, does not in any significant way reveal designative signification. Nor does it serve, in its present form, for the study of prescriptive signification. We have seen that there are relations between Osgood's factors and the designative and appraisive dimensions of signification, but no simple parallel. So while the present model of dimensions of signification is not simply reproduced by Osgood's results, these results give no grounds for abandoning the model. They do suggest the need for clarification of 'connotative meaning' and for further experimental studies for controlling the model.

---

[6] John B. Carroll, review of Osgood's *The Measurement of Meaning*, in *Language* 35 (1959), pp. 58-77.

[7] Arthur W. Staats, "Use of the Semantic Differential in Research on S-R Mediational Principles of Learning Word Meaning," paper presented at Western Psychological Association, San Diego, California, April 1959.

One additional query may be raised: What is the relation of the Osgood factors to the five (or six) value dimensions which were isolated and discussed in Chapter 2? Intuitively, it may seem that the relation here is closer than in the case of the dimensions of signification. Osgood's receptivity factor seems to have much in common with the value factor *E* (sensuous enjoyment), his factors "potency" and "activity" with the value factor *B* (progress and enjoyment through action), and his "stability" factor with value factor *A* (social restraint and self-control).

A study made by Osgood, Edward E. Ware, and myself[8] to relate Osgood's results with my value results did not, however, throw much light on these intuitively suggested relations. It is evident that much further study is needed in this area.

§ 5. SEMIOTIC, AXIOLOGY, AND THE SOCIAL SCIENCES

Talcott Parsons and his coauthor Edward Shils have remarked that "There is probably no problem in the analysis of action systems which would not be greatly clarified by a better understanding of symbolism."[9] Since then, Parsons and his co-workers Edward Shils and Robert Bales have been increasingly concerned with this area, and their *Working Papers in the Theory of Action*[10] is, among other things, an explicit attempt to bring the theory of signs into their theory of action. It seems to me that the results of their independent analysis are for the most part in harmony with the position taken in the present study, and thus offer some support for this model. At the same time, I believe that this semiotic can at certain points sharpen, or at least clarify, their analysis.

---

[8] Charles E. Osgood, Edward E. Ware, and Charles Morris, "Analysis of the Connotative Meanings of a Variety of Human Values as Expressed by American College Students," *Journal of Abnormal and Social Psychology* 62 (1961), pp. 62-73.

[9] Talcott Parsons and Edward A. Shils, "Values, Motives, and Systems of Action," in *Toward a General Theory of Action*, T. Parsons and E. A. Shils, eds. (Cambridge, Mass.: Harvard University Press, 1951), p. 242.

[10] Talcott Parsons, Robert F. Bales, and Edward A. Shils, *Working Papers in the Theory of Action* (Glencoe, Ill.: The Free Press, 1953). See especially Chapter 2, "The Theory of Symbolism in Relation to Action."

Semiotic, Axiology, and the Social Sciences

In the Parsonian analysis, human action is a system that contains three subsystems: the personality system, the social system, and the cultural system. Since the organism is, however, part of human action, the diagram of Figure 2 is permissible.[11] These

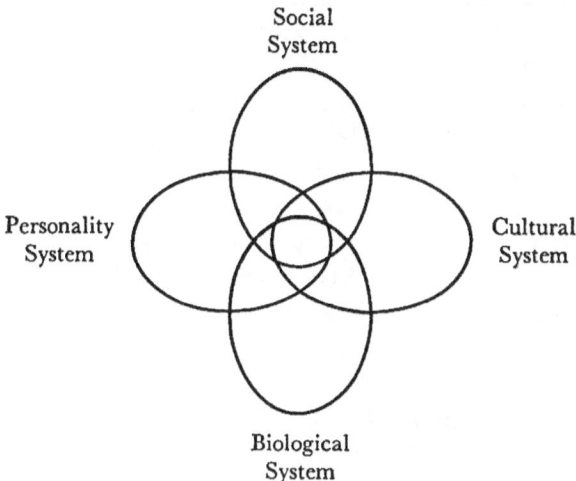

FIGURE 2. Human Action System

systems are regarded as irreducible subsystems of human action. In our terms, each has its own boundary-maintaining devices. In other words, neither psychology, sociology, anthropology, nor human biology alone can give the whole account of human action, nor can any one of these disciplines be reduced to another.

Furthermore, it is recognized that signs (and values) play an important role in the origin, maintenance, and nature of these subsystems, and hence in human action as a whole. Thus a cultural system is defined in Parsons's *The Social System* as "a shared symbol system which functions in interaction."[12] It differs from a social system, which is a system of interactions, since a cultural system may function in many social systems (Buddhism, Christianity, and mathematics are examples of this). I shall concentrate my attention here upon Parsons's position in *The Social System*.

In the analysis given in his work, social systems are regarded

---

[11] From my comments in *Toward a Unified Theory of Human Behavior*, Roy R. Grinker, ed. (New York: Basic Books, 1956), pp. 350-351.
[12] Talcott Parsons, *The Social System* (Glencoe, Ill.: The Free Press, 1951), p. 11.

as organizations of institutions (such as the family, churches, markets); institutions are regarded as systems of roles (such as the roles of father, mother, and children in the family); and roles are regarded as systems of complementary expectations (as when a son has certain expectations about the behavior of his father as a father and the father has certain expectations about the behavior of his son as a son).

Such expectations are of course sign processes and have interpretants and significations. Hence, signs in this analysis turn out to be the central features of social systems.[13] Accordingly, the theory of signs becomes of basic importance to sociology. One test of a semiotic is whether it will assist the sociologist, as the student of social systems, in his detailed analysis.

To take an example of the complexities of the issues involved, let us consider the role of policeman. It will be helpful first to make a distinction between prelinguistic, linguistic, and postlinguistic signs. *Prelinguistic signs* are those which occur in the child's behavior before it speaks, or which later, even in the adult, are independent of language signs. *Linguistic signs* are those which occur in a language considered as a system of interpersonal signs restricted in their possibility of combination. *Postlinguistic signs* are signs which owe their signification to language but which are not themselves elements of language. The carved bear on a totem pole, the flag of a nation, the perception of a star as a large distant flaming object, and the policeman's badge are examples of postlinguistic signs.

In our culture, the term 'policeman' has designative, appraisive, and prescriptive dimensions. A person who is denoted by this sign, and so performs the role of a policeman, is expected to act in certain ways under certain conditions, is regarded as important in his work, is regarded as a person of whom certain types of behavior are expected. The person acting as policeman also expects certain types of behavior from others with respect to his own role behavior. Thus the term 'policeman', in Parsonian terminology, involves a set of "complementary expectations."

---

[13] See also Radhakamal Mukerjee, *The Symbolic Life of Man* (Bombay: Hind Kitabs Ltd., 1959); Lloyd Warner, *The Living and the Dead* (New Haven: Yale University Press, 1959); Hugh Dalziel Duncan, *Communication and Social Order*, second edition (Totowa, N.J.: Bedminster Press, 1956).

In terms of the present analysis, these complementary expectations which make up the role of a policeman are sign processes, whose signs to the policeman and to other members of the society have a common designative, appraisive, and prescriptive signification—a policeman is one who is to react in certain ways under certain conditions and to whom other persons are to react in certain ways under these conditions. The term 'policeman' may then be called a "comsign," since it has a common signification to those who produce it and to other persons who interpret it. This signification is then extended to the uniform and to the badge as postlinguistic signs. Hence, role behavior is a type of sign-controlled behavior, and such behavior is central to a social system conceived as a set of institutions which in turn are conceived as systems of roles.

Let us consider some aspects of Parsons's treatment of expectancies. Roles (such as being a policeman) involve, as we have seen, "complementary-expectancies." Such expectancies are called "role-expectancies" by Parsons. They differ in certain respects from the wider class of expectations, "for among the expectations of any role, indeed the central part of them, are definitions of how its incumbent should act toward others. . . ."[14] Now if we take "definition," as it obviously should be taken in this context, as wider than the logician's usage of the term, then Parsons's role-expectations involve appraisive and prescriptive significations as well as designative. Since they have the same characters in various social interactions, they are "comsigns." In this analysis there is, I believe, nothing that is not found in Parsons; what I have done is merely to try to make more explicit in my terms what is involved in his.

Parsons's approach stresses the situation "as known to the actor in question" in contrast to "the situation as known to or knowable by an observer." In the present approach the distinction is admitted, but the two approaches are regarded as complementary accounts of a single process.

Parsons distinguishes three types of "value-orientations": cognitive, appreciative, and moral. These are related to what I have called the perceptual (and manipulative) stages of the act, the

---

[14] Talcott Parsons, *The Social System* (Glencoe, Ill.: The Free Press, 1951), p. 40.

consummatory stage, and the process of evaluation. Similarly, Parsons distinguishes three types of symbol system: the cognitive, the expressive, and the normative or regulative (which in turn breaks up into cognitive, appreciative, and moral norms). In terms of the present approach, this is another way of marking the distinction between primarily designative, appraisive, and prescriptive signs and sign systems. Once again, the Parsonian and the present analysis converge in outcome, though they are independent in their historical starting points.

Finally, let us return to Figure 2. The overlapping area of the four ellipses is predominantly the area of comsigns. Comsigns have the same (or similar) signification to those who produce them and to those who interpret them. They are part of the cultural system and operate in both the personality system and the social system (a person becomes and acts as a policeman, and being a policeman is a role in the social system). And if the interpretant of the sign is conceived as a disposition in the organism to respond in a certain way (because of the sign), then the comsign is also anchored in the biological system. Comsigns are thus the integrators of the personality, social, cultural, and biological systems, and hence the integrators of the human action system. Since the main comsigns are linguistic symbols and the postlinguistic signs they make possible, man is indeed "*homo symbolicus.*"[15] Sociology is not indebted to semiotic for this insight, but a stricter and more expanded semiotic may aid it in the detailed development of this basic insight.

§ 6. A NOTE CONCERNING CONTEMPORARY LINGUISTICS

In *Signs, Language, and Behavior* the very general notion of a *lansign system*[16] was introduced. Such a system is essentially a set of signs with common interpersonal significations, the signs being restricted as to their possible combinations. This notion is very general—it applies to symbolic logic and to mathematics as well as to spoken and written languages, and perhaps to the arts.

---

[15] The term is used by Radhakamal Mukerjee.
[16] Charles Morris, *Signs, Language, and Behavior* (New York: Prentice-Hall, 1946; New York: George Braziller, 1955), pp. 35 ff.

A lansign system may be specified in terms of the syntactical, semantical, and pragmatical rules governing the component signs.[17] The syntactical rules are often divided into formation rules (governing the possible sign combinations) and transformation rules (governing the sign combinations which may be derived from other sign combinations). If only syntactical rules are given, a lansign system is said to be *uninterpreted;* if semantical rules are given, it is said to be *interpreted.* Existing lansign systems may be studied (the natural languages), or lansign systems may be deliberately constructed and then studied (as done by many mathematicians and logicians).

Contemporary linguists usually regard linguistics as the study of spoken languages. Linguistics is conceived of both as *descriptive*, since it studies a corpus of utterances, and as *structural*, since it aims to discover the structural relations between elements in the corpus of utterances. In semiotical terms, the contemporary linguist sharply distinguishes between the study of the syntax of a language and the study of its semantics and pragmatics. The extreme position is the belief that the syntax of a language can be studied in complete independence from its semantical and pragmatical aspects[18]—though it would be admitted that the complete study of a language involves these aspects.

Much of the frontier work in recent linguistics has thus been in the syntactical study of certain lansign systems (namely the spoken languages). There is now a growing movement by professional linguists to extend the study of language to its semantical aspects, to the relation of language to culture, and to certain of its pragmatical aspects.[19]

---

[17] The terminology of this paragraph (except for 'lansign system') draws much from Rudolf Carnap.

[18] Noam Chomsky, *Syntactic Structures* (The Hague: Mouton & Co., 1957).

[19] Floyd G. Lounsbury, "A Semantic Analysis of the Pawnee Kinship Usage," *Language* 32 (1956), pp. 158-194; Ward H. Goodenough, "Componential Analysis and the Study of Meaning," *ibid.*, pp. 195-216; Harry Hoijer, ed., *Language in Culture* (Chicago: University of Chicago Press, 1954); *Psycholinguistics*, Charles E. Osgood and Thomas A. Sebeok, eds., supplement to *International Journal of American Linguistics* 20 (1954); Kenneth L. Pike, *Language in Relation to a Unified Theory of the Structure of Human Behavior*, preliminary edition (Ann Arbor, Mich.: Wahr's University Bookstore, 316 South State Street, Part I, 1954; Part II, 1955; Part III, 1960). For the relation of linguistics to other studies of language and communication, see John B. Carroll, *The Study of Language* (Cam-

There is an interesting parallel between the development of technical linguistics in this century and the development of logic. Rudolf Carnap, for instance, tried at first to see how far he could go with purely syntactical considerations. Then, partly under the influence of the Polish logicians, he extended his studies into the area of semantics. In his recent work he has recognized the necessity, within logic itself, of moving into the area of pragmatics. Carnap has limited his concern to constructed languages, while the linguists deal with actual spoken languages. But the parallel development is clear.

That linguistics is part of semiotic is commonly admitted. Ferdinand de Saussure conceived of linguistics as a part of "semiology."[20] Louis Hjelmslev (in his *Prolegomena to a Theory of Language*)[21] also uses 'semiology' as the general term. His term 'semiotic' is like the term 'lansign system'—a semiotic is "any structure analogous to a language." Leonard Bloomfield[22] also regarded linguistics as a part of semiotic (*Linguistic Aspects of Science*). Joseph Greenberg,[23] in *Essays in Linguistics*, considers "the possibility of a general syntax, of which linguistics would be but a branch." What he calls a "sign system" is similar to what is here called a "lansign system," but he includes the case where only syntactical rules are specified. In the present terminology this would be only the syntactics of a lansign system.

§ 7. A NOTE CONCERNING INFORMATION THEORY

Claude Shannon's 1948 paper and his 1949 book with Warren Weaver, *Mathematical Theory of Communication*,[24] led to exten-

---

bridge, Mass.: Harvard University Press, 1953); Colin Cherry, *On Human Communication: A Review, a Survey, and a Criticism* (Cambridge, Mass.: The Technology Press of the Massachusetts Institute of Technology; New York: John Wiley & Sons, 1957).

[20] Ferdinand de Saussure, *Course in General Linguistics*, translated from the 5th French edition by Wade Baskin (New York: Philosophical Library, 1959).

[21] Louis Hjelmslev, *Prolegomena to a Theory of Language*, revised translation by Francis J. Whitfield (Madison, Wisc.: University of Wisconsin Press, 1961).

[22] Leonard Bloomfield, "Linguistic Aspects of Science," in *International Encyclopedia of Unified Science*, Vol. 1, No. 4 (Chicago: University of Chicago Press, 1939).

[23] Joseph Greenberg, *Essays in Linguistics* (Chicago: University of Chicago Press, 1957).

[24] Claude Shannon and Warren Weaver, *Mathematical Theory of Communication* (Urbana, Ill.: University of Illinois Press, 1949).

sive developments which pose certain terminological problems for a general theory of signs. In the United States this development came to be known as "information theory." In England it is more wisely called "communication theory," because the technical term 'information' in the Shannon approach differs widely from certain everyday usages of the term. Our interest here is not with the general theory itself but only with its relation to semiotic.

It is now generally recognized that "information theory" is not a rival to, or a substitute for, a general theory of signs. It was developed by engineers concerned with the most efficient way to transmit messages. Their concern is with the transmission of any message whatever, independent of the content of the message. If we call the sign independent of its signification a *sign-vehicle*, the Shannon type of "information theory" is a theory of efficient sign-vehicle transmission, and not a general theory of signs. It is part of the pragmatical and syntactical portions of semiotic—pragmatical in that it is concerned with efficient transmission of sign-vehicles, and syntactical in that it considers the sign-vehicles alone in abstraction from their significations or their uses.

The situation was clarified in a paper by Y. Bar-Hillel, "An Examination of Information Theory," in 1955,[25] and in earlier papers by D. M. MacKay in *Cybernetics: Transactions of the Eighth Congress*,[26] and "Operational Aspects of Some Fundamental Concepts of Human Communications."[27]

MacKay distinguishes between selective and semantic information. Information in general he regards as that which changes our "representations," i.e., our signs. Thus to gain information is to have a change in our expectations (our dispositions to respond) caused by a sign. Selective information gives the information necessary to select the message itself (the set of sign-vehicles) from a possible set of messages, and it is not concerned with the content (the signification) of the message. Semantic information

---

[25] Y. Bar-Hillel, "An Examination of Information Theory," *Philosophy of Science* 22 (1955), pp. 86-103.
[26] D. M. MacKay, "In Search of Basic Symbols" and "The Nomenclature of Information Theory," in *Cybernetics: Transactions of the Eighth Congress*, Heinz von Foerster, ed. (New York: Macy Foundation, 1952).
[27] D. M. MacKay, "Operational Aspects of Some Fundamental Concepts of Human Communications," *Synthese* 9, pp. 183-198.

is concerned with the content (the signification) of the message. "Information" of the Shannon variety is selective information only and has nothing to do with the signification of the message. The mathematical treatment of selective information has proved to be very important, but it is not a general theory of signs.

The current widespread usages of 'information' and 'communication' raise some terminological problems with respect to a semiotical framework. There are various possible decisions. We could limit these terms to cases where messages with signification occur. Or we could extend the range of denotation of these terms to cases where signification is not involved, as in thermostats. Or (and this seems desirable in the light of the present work) we could extend the denotation of 'communication' and 'information' beyond semiotic but limit semiotic to processes involving signification and hence interpretants. If this usage were followed, both semiosical and nonsemiosical systems might occur in inorganic nature. The differences in sign behavior in nonliving and living systems would in this case be a matter of the degree of complexity involved. This would hold true also for the differences in living systems. In the linguists' sense of 'language', no animals other than men are known to have languages.

The term 'signal' is in common usage in engineering, neurology, and the studies of animal behavior. Thus N. Tinbergen speaks of "the signaling behavior of gulls."[28] Certainly many of the "signals" referred to in engineering and neurological studies are not signs in the sense of the present study. But since 'sign' has not been defined here in the strict sense, it would be possible to develop a semiotic which included such "signals" as signs. The question of the lower limit of sign behavior becomes an empirical problem only after one has decided upon the criterion of sign behavior, and this can be done in various ways. I have tended to restrict semiotic to the study of behavior involving significations and interpretants, and to make signals a kind of sign—but this is only one possible usage. Another alternative would be to let 'signal', like 'information' and 'communication', roam beyond the borders of semiotic.

---

[28] N. Tinbergen, "The Evolution of Behavior in Gulls," *Scientific American*, 1960, pp. 118 ff.

5

Art, Signs, and Values

§ 1. THE ISSUES

If we consider aesthetics to be the study of art, in what sense and to what degree can semiotic and axiology contribute to aesthetics?

On the face of it, it is plain that art can in many ways be talked about in terms of signs and value. Discussions constantly raise the question of the "meaning" of a work of art. There are few persons who would say that a work of art or at least that all works of art are "meaningless," but the sense in which a work of art is affirmed to be "meaningful" is seldom clear. Semiotic and axiology as here conceived seem to be potentially valuable disciplines for dealing with such a problem, for they force us to distinguish between the questions of whether a work of art has signification (i.e., is or is not a sign) and whether it has (and how it has) significance or value. With respect to signification, the distinctions between designative, appraisive, and prescriptive signification are important in the analysis of art. With respect to significance, the distinctions between operative, conceived, and object values are relevant. Insofar as the work of art is a sign or at least includes signs within itself, aesthetics, as the study of art, has semantical and syntactical aspects, and insofar as aesthetics deals also with the origin, uses, and effects of works of art, it has its pragmatic aspect. The differences among theorists often depend in large part upon which aspects of the art situation are stressed.

If all works of art are signs, then aesthetics becomes part of semiotic. If no works of art are signs or include signs, semiotic is irrelevant for aesthetics. If some works of art are signs or include signs, semiotic is to that extent applicable within aesthetics. Regardless of whether works of art are signs or include signs, discussions of their significance involve axiology.

All of these alternatives are represented in current discussions of art. It is held by some that the work of art is a sign and by others that it is not; it is held by some that the work of art somehow presents values and by others that it does not; it is held by some that the disciplines of semiotic and axiology provide the proper metalanguage for aesthetics and by others that the everyday language by itself or when supplemented by the language of aesthetic criticism is the most adequate way to talk about art.

§ 2. ONE APPROACH TO THESE ISSUES

In an article in 1939 entitled "Esthetics and the Theory of Signs,"[1] I maintained two extreme positions: first, that the work of art is a sign and hence that aesthetics is part of semiotic; second, that it is possible to differentiate the aesthetic sign from other signs by the joint application of semiotical and axiological concepts.

This article has been much discussed in the intervening years, defended in some respects, and subjected to sharp negative criticism in other respects.[2] Some of the issues raised are worth considering here, not as a defense of the position taken in the 1939 article, but because these issues are central to the topic of this chapter: the relation of art, signs, and values.

That the work of art in general is not a sign is the position of Richard Rudner and Kingsley Price;[3] that, while signs occur

---

[1] Charles Morris, "Esthetics and the Theory of Signs," *Journal of Unified Science (Erkenntnis)* 8 (1939), pp. 131-150.

[2] For a survey of some of the reactions, see Charles Morris and Daniel J. Hamilton, "Aesthetics, Signs, and Icons," to appear in *Journal of Philosophy and Phenomenological Research.*

[3] Richard Rudner, "On Semiotic Aesthetics," *Journal of Aesthetics and Art Criticism* 10 (1951), p. 66-77; Kingsley Blake Price, "Is a Work of Art a Symbol?" *Journal of Philosophy* 50 (1953), pp. 485-503.

in the representational arts, nonrepresentational works of art (such as pure music, nonrepresentational paintings) exist and are not signs is the position of Abraham Kaplan and Charles Stevenson.[4] Thus in these views semiotic either is not relevant to aesthetics or at best is relevant to the analysis and understanding of the signs which occur in the representational arts.

I should not care to argue now that the work of art is always a sign, but the arguments against this position do not seem to me to be compelling. Roughly, they say that if a work of art is a sign, then it must "refer" to something other than itself; but if this is so, we cannot distinguish the work of art from any other representational process, such as a scientific treatise.

The difficulty lies in the term 'refer'. In the semiotic developed here it is true that a sign must in a sense "signify something." Thus a sign must have signification, but it need not *denote* anything. A drawing of a centaur signifies a certain kind of animal, and one can pay attention to this signification without there being any centaurs. It must be granted, however, that this consideration does not in itself distinguish a work of art from, say, a blueprint of an unbuilt house.

Further, "to be a sign" is a vague expression. It may include the requirement of "making a statement about," or it may not. The drawing of a centaur does not "assert" centaurs. If one wanted to say that the drawing does "make statements," clearly this means no more than that the drawing exhibits some characteristics something must possess to be called a centaur (i.e., to be denoted by the term 'centaur'). In any case, the drawing can signify (and in *this* sense be a sign) without denoting anything.

I think it can be maintained that at least some nonrepresentational works of art signify and are signs in the sense that the drawing of the centaur is a sign. But this point will not be argued here.[5]

---

[4] Abraham Kaplan, "Referential Meaning in the Arts," *Journal of Aesthetics and Art Criticism* 12 (1954), pp. 457-474; Charles L. Stevenson, "Symbolism in the Nonrepresentational Arts," in *Language, Thought, and Culture*, P. Henle ed. (Ann Arbor: University of Michigan Press, 1958), pp. 196-225.

[5] In this chapter I am not raising the important question of how far sign processes occur within the sign-vehicle itself—even if the work of art as a whole is not a sign. That such sign relations do occur is shown in Benbow Ritchie's article

68   *Art, Signs, and Values*

§ 3. THE AESTHETIC SIGN AS AN ICON

The preceding analysis, even if acceptable, does not isolate the aesthetic sign or bring in questions of value. In my 1939 article I dealt with these matters in terms of the concept of "iconic sign." An iconic sign is one which would denote any object having certain properties it possesses itself. Thus the drawing of a centaur is an iconic sign in this sense. It is not solely an iconic sign, however. The interpreter of such a drawing may say it signifies an animal that has a body and a head like those drawn but is also alive and has flesh and bones. The drawing itself is not alive nor does it have flesh and bones. Iconicity is thus a matter of degree. Its lower limits would be found in the case where the sign-vehicle had nothing in common with its possible denotata (such as the word 'cross' when used to signify the cross of the crucifixion); and its upper limit would be found in the case where the iconic sign-vehicle had all the properties of what it denoted. The latter case makes it clear that mere similarity of two objects does not as such make one of them an iconic sign of the other. Reproductions of the drawing of the centaur would not as such be iconic signs of each other—each would signify a centaur. Only in very special cases would a reproduction be an iconic sign of the original drawing—as when the interpreter of a reproduction interprets it as a sign of the original. An iconic sign, like every sign, must have an interpretant.

It is also true that the same sign-vehicle can have different significations in different sign processes. Thus the mark '+' could be a sign of a cross or a sign of the mathematical operation *plus*. And various drawings of centaurs might be signs to an art historian of various styles of art, or even of various artists.

These remarks on iconic signs have gone beyond the treatment of the iconic sign in the 1939 article, largely in reaction to criticisms of that article. In their totality these remarks even question a central point of that article, namely the claim that an iconic sign is unique among signs in that it denotes itself—i.e., the sign-

---

"The Formal Structure of the Aesthetic Object," *Journal of Aesthetics and Art Criticism* 3 (1944), pp. 5-14; and in Leonard Meyer's *Emotion and Meaning in Music* (Chicago: University of Chicago Press, 1956).

vehicle itself has the properties which are signified. Thus in this view the drawing of a centaur itself has properties that a centaur would have and so falls among the items it could denote. I think it is too early to accept or reject this position completely. The attractiveness of such a position for an explanation of aesthetic perception is obvious. For the work of art can signify, but its perceiver need not be distracted from giving his sole attention to the work of art since all that is signified is actually embodied in the work of art itself. There are important elements of truth in this analysis, but in terms of what we have said about iconic signs it is certainly too simple. For if we mean by the work of art the sign-vehicle itself, some but not all of the qualities that are signified are present in the sign-vehicle—as we saw in the case of the drawing of a centaur. The iconicity may here be very slight. If we mean by the work of art the sign-vehicle operating as a sign, then it is no longer helpful to say that what is signified is iconically embodied (and hence denoted) in the work of art. The aesthetic perception of this complex situation may be characteristically different from other forms of perception. But this is another problem, and I no longer feel that its solution is aided by saying that all iconic signs denote themselves. It seems semiotically neater to say that all signs signify but that no sign necessarily denotes. I prefer, however, not to make a decision on this point here.[6]

§ 4. THE AESTHETIC SIGN AND VALUES

There are two kinds of questions concerning the relation of values and art. One concerns the nature of aesthetic evaluation. No special problems seem to arise here that cannot be dealt with in the analysis of inquiry given in Chapter 2. Aesthetic inquiry differs from other forms of inquiry only in its subject matter, namely works of art. Inquiry about works of art can be designative, appraisive, or prescriptive, and schools of "criticism" differ mainly in the relative stress given to these forms of inquiry.

The other problem concerns the relation of the work of art

---

[6] This problem arises in another form in the analysis of analytic formative ascriptors in symbolic logic and mathematics.

itself to values. The position of the 1939 article was that the work of art signified values and that in its iconic character it embodied in itself the values it signified. Thus I proposed that the aesthetic sign iconically signifies values.

At that time, no reference was made to the distinctions between operative, conceived, and object values. The aesthetic sign does not signify its own object value (e.g., its capacity to reinforce perception of it), for that is a metalinguistic statement about the work of art. Nevertheless, a work of art can in some cases signify object values of some object that it signifies. Thus a painting showing a number of people obviously enjoying a given beverage is some evidence that the beverage is signified as having positive value. Similarly, the work of art can portray both operative and conceived values. The character in a novel reveals by his or her signified actions the values that are "actually" operative in the course of this person's signified preferential behavior. As for conceived values, the utopias signify someone's conception of a society that would be preferred to other societies if it could be attained. And religious paintings and literature portray, among other things, the kind of persons held desirable in the religion.

Thus not only can the work of art, verbal or nonverbal, signify designatively, appraisively, and prescriptively, but it can portray or embody operative, conceived, and object values; and like other human products, it can be used for many purposes. The verbal arts are of great importance, but one of the important tasks of semiotic is to see that full justice is done to preverbal signs, "verbal" sign systems not based on spoken words, and postverbal signs.

§ 5. ART AS THE EMBODIMENT OR PORTRAYAL OF VALUES

In my 1939 article, I stated that the value properties in the work of art "stand out" for inspection, and the perceiver therefore has a "direct apprehension" of such value properties. A number of critics, such as Allen Tate,[7] find it difficult to under-

---

[7] Allen Tate, *Reason in Madness* (New York: G. P. Putnam's Sons, 1941), pp. 20-62.

stand what is meant by such terms. Tate's own belief is that some act of cognition is involved in such matters, and that the whole approach is defective in not dealing with the place of cognition in the perception of a work of art. Whether explicitly dealing with "cognition" would or would not be the way out, Tate is certainly right that further analysis is needed concerning the way in which the work of art embodies values and how these values are apprehended.

In the treatment of value in Chapter 2, values were approached in terms of preferential behavior. A value situation was regarded as a situation where preferential behavior was (somewhat consistently) accorded to something present in the situation or to something not present but signified in the situation. Values were thus said to be "objectively relative"—they were properties of objects (including signs and signified objects) relative to preferential behavior. "Edibility" was given as an example of another objectively relative property—certain objects are edible but only in relation to certain kinds of digestive systems.

If this is so, in what sense can a work of art "embody" a value, and in what sense can there be a "direct apprehension" of such a value? Let us take an example. Suppose a given person likes strong, vigorous persons and chooses such persons as his greatest friends and heroes. He is given a set of paintings portraying many kinds of persons. When asked to rate the paintings in terms of how much he likes them, he is found to prefer those paintings which portray strong and active persons. He may also admit that such persons conform to his ideal of what persons should be. Strong and active persons, in relation to his preferential behavior, have operative, conceived, and object value. The paintings that he likes represent persons with these values, and to the extent that they are iconic the painted persons are themselves strong and active (i.e., we apply in our everyday language such terms as 'strong' and 'active' to them). To this extent the values are "embodied" in the paintings; and while the phrase "directly apprehended" is not very helpful, the values are directly apprehended in that they are there directly in the situation, and not merely signified.

This does not mean that the values in question are not also

signified insofar as the work of art is a sign. The 1939 article maintained that in aesthetic perception there is both an immediate and a mediated taking account of value. The work of art involves both a sign-vehicle and its functioning as a sign. The sign portrays values mediately, while the sign-vehicle presents the same values immediately.

Another way of dealing with the problem of combining mediation and immediacy is described by Charles Stevenson.[8] He holds that if the interpretant of the aesthetic sign process is considered as a disposition to respond rather than an actual response (and that is the position taken here), then the work of art, to the extent that it involves an interpretant, is functioning as a sign (is mediational); and at the same time it results in no overt behavior to something else, and is to that extent immediate.

§ 6. SUPPLEMENTARY APPROACHES

We have been concerned with the discussions and criticisms of the hypothesis that the work of art is an iconic sign signifying values. It still seems to me that this line of thought is a powerful one and is important for aesthetics. But there are supplementary, and perhaps alternative, approaches to the problem.

The 1939 article did not operate in terms of the distinction between the dimensions of signification, or the distinction between the signification and the uses of a sign. In the brief discussion of art in *Signs, Language, and Behavior*, I suggested that aesthetic discourse (there called, too narrowly, poetic discourse) was the type of discourse where signs were appraisive in signification and were used to elicit from the interpreter positive preferential behavior to what was signified and to the signs themselves by which it was signified. Thus a Whitman poem on death signifies death as having a high positive significance and is used to evoke in the reader a disposition to favor the poem itself and the attitude to death that it signifies. It is of course not essential that the reader permanently adopt this attitude to death, but in the reading of

---

[8] Charles L. Stevenson, "Symbolism in the Representational Arts," in *Language, Thought, and Culture*, P. Henle ed. (Ann Arbor: University of Michigan Press, 1958), pp. 226-257.

the poem this attitude must be aroused as a disposition if the poem is to be understood.

This suggested approach to aesthetic discourse does not attempt to isolate a special class of aesthetic signs—any appraisive sign can be used for aesthetic purposes. Nor does this approach require that aesthetic discourse be iconic, though it does not exclude this possibility or deny that iconic signs may play an especially significant role in aesthetic discourse. Only if one denies that aesthetic discourse is, in important respects, iconic would this approach, taken in *Signs, Language, and Behavior*, be a clear alternative to the thesis of the 1939 article. Otherwise, it simply supplements that thesis by bringing in the category of use and by stressing specifically the appraisive dimension of signification.

Another possible approach to the problems of aesthetics via semiotic and axiology would be to attempt to isolate a special form of aesthetic behavior, and then to investigate the relation of such behavior to signs and values. One candidate for such behavior is often called "aesthetic perception." As contrasted to cognitive perception (where the sign is perceived as giving information about something other than itself) and as contrasted to practical perception (where the sign is responded to as a way of accomplishing some purpose), aesthetic perception is "for its own sake." What is perceived aesthetically may, but need not, be a sign. The signs that do occur in aesthetic perception need not be iconic, need not be limited to any single dimension of signification (such as the appraisive), and need not be given some primary use (such as the valuative). The relation of signs and values to aesthetic perception is then an open study, and semiotic and axiology are simply agencies in this study.

§ 7. EXPERIMENTAL POSSIBILITIES

Given the isolation of dimensions of value, and scales of measurement for these dimensions, and given a (much more hypothetical) analysis of "dimensions" of signification, one can plan a variety of experimental studies of the relation of signs and values in the arts.

For example, a number of persons could rate on a seven-point scale how much they liked several paintings, poems, pieces of music, and so forth. We may call these P-ratings, or Preference Ratings. These persons could also be asked to evaluate or appraise the same objects as works of art, perhaps also on a seven-point scale. We may call these A-ratings, or Appraisive Ratings. (Since these are, of course, not limited to art, the 'A' does not signify art ratings.) The persons may also give P- and A-ratings to ways to live, to extracts from different philosophies, and the like.

If a number of judges analyzed some of these items in semiotical terms (syntactically, semantically, and pragmatically), it would then be possible to study in great detail the relation of significance and signification in works of art.

If additional data on the subjects who gave the P- and A-ratings were obtained (constitutional traits, temperamental traits, cultural affiliation, economic status, sex, etc.), it would also be possible to study the relation of the ratings to those who made the ratings.

A vast field for exploration can thus be discerned. The results of such exploration would be relevant to all phases of aesthetics —the more philosophic as well as the more scientific aspects.

The use of modern statistical analysis (such as factor analysis) would permit the empirical determination of which paintings "went with" (in terms of ratings) which poems, which music, which ways to live, which philosophies, and which religions. The resulting clusters might well include such traditional styles as "classical" and "romantic," but might well go beyond the traditional classifications—there might be styles corresponding to all of the ways to live, or to all of the value dimensions, or to each of the three categories of dependence, dominance, and detachment.

The same data might also be used in the study of the relation between preferences (P-ratings) and appraisals (A-ratings). It could also be used in cross-cultural studies, in the comparisons of various groups in a single culture, and in the study of individual differences. The possibilities are indeed very great.

§ 8. EXPERIMENTAL STUDIES

The "grand scale" investigation suggested in § 7 has not been made. Nevertheless, over a period of some fifteen years, the author has worked to some extent on all of the major problems posed. The "grand scale" investigation was not possible at the time that work began, since a factor analysis of such magnitude was not feasible until the development of computing machines. Moreover, it is not possible to make the investigation now with the original data, since the data were not collected with this end in view; hence, many groups were studied in which only some of the requisite data were obtained. The results are reported mainly in *Varieties of Human Value,* "Significance, Signification, and Painting," and "Paintings, Ways to Live, and Values."[9] Here only some general results and observations need be given.

As the titles just mentioned indicate, a major emphasis in these studies has been the comparison of the ratings of the thirteen ways to live with the ratings of certain paintings. The ratings compared were in most cases P-ratings on a scale from seven to one, but in some cases A-ratings were used.

The paintings were colored reproductions, usually about letter size. Eighty such reproductions were used, but the main work was done on a selected set of twenty reproductions. The paintings were made, for the most part, in the nineteenth and twentieth centuries. All of them portray persons and things. In this sense they are iconic.

At the time the studies were done, the five value dimensions had not been abstracted by factor analysis. And since many of the persons who rated the paintings did not rate the ways to live, the data do not permit us now to determine by factor analysis which ways to live and which paintings go together in the ratings. Nevertheless, something of this sort can be determined, since both the ways to live and the paintings had been ranked by judges as to the extent they portrayed the values of dependence (or receptivity), dominance, and detachment. Since some subjects also rated both the ways to live and the paintings, it is possible to get some idea as to how the acceptance of the values embodied in the ways

---

[9] Charles Morris, *Varieties of Human Value* (Chicago: University of Chicago Press, 1956), Chap. 7; Charles Morris, "Significance, Signification, and Paintings," in *The Language of Value,* R. Lepley, ed. (New York: Columbia University Press, 1956); Charles Morris and Frank Sciadini, "Paintings, Ways to Live, and Values," to appear in a series of volumes on the visual arts, edited by Gyorgy Kepes.

to live is related to the liking or the appraisal of the paintings portraying certain values.

The relation, as one would suspect, is in general positive. By and large, persons like and positively appraise those paintings portraying the values of dependence, dominance, and detachment (as rated by a set of judges) found in the ways to live which they like and positively appraise. And the same is true with respect to disliking and negative appraisals. Since it was also found that usually acceptance or rejection of the ways to live was positively related to constitutional and temperamental characteristics of the subjects (using, respectively, W. H. Sheldon's constitutional and L. L. Thurstone's temperament categories), the acceptance or rejection of paintings usually depends on the values they portray as related to the values of the subjects who judge them.

A clear example is found in the case of persons liking Way 2 or Way 5. Way 2 stresses detachment, self-sufficiency, reflectiveness, heightened self-awareness; Way 5 stresses mergence with the social group, social action and enjoyment, social dominance. This contrast is the greatest found among the ways to live: liking of Way 2 tends strongly to go along with dislike of Way 5, and vice versa.

The same opposition appears in the liking of the paintings. The pictures which were differentially preferred by those who liked Way 2 more than by those who liked other ways, were differentially liked least by those who liked Way 5.[10] The pictures liked by Way 2 persons were rated by the judges as highest in detachment, next in dependence, and lowest in dominance (and Way 2 was rated similarly by the judges).[11] Way 5 was rated by the judges as highest in dominance, next in dependence, and lowest in detachment.[12]

Many more instances could be given of this tendency to favor works of art signifying the values which one holds. It is believed that this is true of the producer of the work of art as well as other perceivers of it, though this aspect was not investigated in our study. Nevertheless, a word of caution is now necessary.

---

[10] *Varieties of Human Value, op. cit.*, Table 69, p. 160.
[11] *Ibid.*, Table 70, p. 161.
[12] *Ibid.*, Table 3, p. 29.

§ 9. SOME FURTHER CONSIDERATIONS

So far in talking about art, I have usually not taken account of the differentiation of operative, conceived, and object values.

The work of art has object value to the extent that it continues (or might continue) to support positive preferential behavior or, as others might say, to the extent that it continues (or might continue) to give satisfaction to its perceivers. With respect to the category of object value, the work of art seems to present no unique problems.

As we have observed before, a person's conceived values may be in various degrees of harmony or disharmony with his operative values. And the same may be true of the practices and ideals of a group or an entire social system. Operative values are in the main congruent with conceived values; otherwise, persons and societies would not be the going concerns that they are. But this is true only "in the main," for in all persons and societies there are some tensions between operative and conceived values, and these tensions may be so great that the working of the system is disturbed, and the system may even be disrupted.

These considerations are relevant to the field of art. On the whole, as we have seen, the subjects' preferences for the paintings tended to go along with their appraisals of them as works of art (i.e., the P-ratings correlated positively with the A-ratings).[13] If a person's conceived value for a work of art is merely that he likes it, then if he is consistent, his A-ratings should coincide with his P-ratings. If a person holds that the extent to which he likes something is evidence of the degree of aesthetic "badness" of that thing, then his A-ratings should be the direct negatives of his P-ratings. These two extremes seldom, if ever, occur, but in-between cases do occur and raise interesting problems.

Chinese students gave P-ratings to the thirteen ways to live and also to a number of the colored reproductions of Chinese and Western paintings. They favored ways to live which stressed dominance and activity (Ways 5 and 6), but they did not favor the paintings which portrayed such values. Here is evidence of a discrepancy between values in the selection of the ways to live

---

[13] The correlation is .64.

and values in the selection of the paintings. These students were, on the whole, sympathetic to the Communist ideology, and conceptually they valued active participation in the reconstruction of China. But they were at the time still Chinese students, and the pictures they liked did not portray the values advocated in the ways to live that they liked.

In Chapter 2, five value dimensions were isolated from an analysis of the P-ratings of thirteen ways to live. These were: Factor A, social restraint and self-control; Factor B, enjoyment and progress through action; Factor C, withdrawal and self-sufficiency; Factor D, receptivity and sympathetic concern; Factor E, indulgence (or sensuous enjoyment). Five ways to live, each the highest on one of the five value dimensions, were used in a study made at the University of Florida with the collaboration of Mr. Frank Sciadini.[14] We selected five paintings that, we thought, "matched" each of the five ways to live, i.e., signified and exemplified the corresponding value. The pictures selected for the five value dimensions were: Factor A, Seurat's *La grande Jatte*; Factor B, Géricault's *Chasseur Officer on Horseback, Charging*; Factor C, Picasso's *The Tragedy*; Factor D, Constable's *Wivenhoe Park, Essex*; Factor E, Brueghel's *Peasant Wedding*.

Two groups of students were asked to describe the ways to live and the paintings in terms of a set of Osgood's semantic scales, to indicate their likings of the ways to live and paintings (P-ratings), and to evaluate the ways to live and the paintings (A-ratings). One group was composed of 68 students in a general course in psychology; the other group of 38 students was composed of persons taking at least one course in art, and many of them were majoring in art.

The two groups agreed closely in the descriptions of the ways to live and the paintings. The descriptions of the ways to live corresponded closely to the paintings that, we believed, would "match" the ways to live. In each group, the order of values as determined by the average P-rating of the five ways to live corresponded to the order of values as determined by the average P-rating of the paintings. Thus if dominance was valued in the ways to live

---

[14] See Note 9 of this chapter.

that a group favored, paintings embodying and portraying dominance were valued by the group. The less artistically oriented group liked and evaluated the paintings in practically the same order, but in the more artistically oriented group, the order of evaluation of the paintings was *practically the reverse* of the order of their preferences for the paintings. In the latter case, the conceived values by which the paintings were judged as works of art differed markedly from the operative values involved directly in liking or disliking the paintings. Hence, liking and appraisal of paintings do not always coincide.

§ 10. ART AND HUMAN BEHAVIOR

Following George H. Mead, we made a distinction in Chapter 1 between the perceptual, manipulatory, and consummatory stages of activity. Where do the art object and its experience fit into this scheme?

Mead, in a provocative article, "The Nature of Aesthetic Experience," stressed the relation of aesthetic experience to the consummation of the act: "To so construct the object that it shall catch this joy of consummation is the achievement of the artist. . . . What is peculiar to it is its power to catch the enjoyment that belongs to the consummation, the outcome, of an undertaking."[15]

In this way the aesthetic experience is a penetration of the consummatory stage of the act into stages of the act earlier than the actual consummation. The whole act gains something of the consummatory quality.

Mead, in this account, is clearly connecting the aesthetic experience and the work of art with values, since values are for him properties that are objectively relative to the consummatory phase of the act. And while Mead here does not talk about the work of art as a sign, its power to bring the consummatory phase

---

[15] George H. Mead, "The Nature of Aesthetic Experience," *Ethics* 36 (1926), pp. 384-387, reprinted in part in George H. Mead, *The Philosophy of the Act* (Chicago: University of Chicago Press, 1938), pp. 454-457. The quotation is from pages 454 and 455 of the latter work.

of the act into earlier stages of the act gives to it, in our terminology, a sign status.

The work of art is a perceived object; the artist manipulates a medium; the perceiver of the work has an experience of consummation. The creation and perception of works of art are human actions[16] and cannot be located within any single stage of action.

Nothing in this chapter or in Mead's article limits the task of the artist to the embodiment in some medium of values already held by the artist or his audience. This is of course part of the great significance of art, as well as its dominant role in traditional cultures. But human activity may seek new directions and new consummations, and art not only may celebrate attained values but may explore and present for our consideration new values.[17] To this extent art plays a dynamic role in the development and integration of human values.

---

[16] See also the writings of Kenneth Burke on art as a form of symbolic actvity. Burke reviewed Mead's books but did not know him personally.

[17] Charles Morris, "Man-Cosmos Symbols," in *The New Landscape in Art and Science*, Gyorgy Kepes (Chicago: Paul Theobald & Co., 1956), pp. 98-99. The whole volume is relevant to this topic.

6

Signs, Values, and Personality Disturbances

Language and the postlinguistic symbols made possible by language are distinctive features of human action. In their designative dimension they embody man's knowledge of the world and of himself; in their appraisive dimension they reflect the conceived values which serve as man's goals; in their prescriptive dimension they direct the specific course of human action toward envisaged goals. Language and postlinguistic symbols are the power and the glory of human life.

Such signs are also the source of much human difficulty.[1] Thomas Hobbes said that man alone has the privilege of absurdity because of his signs. Even worse, because of his signs man, almost alone, has the distress of "mental illness."[2] It is true that

---

[1] See the discussion of personality disturbances in Charles Morris, *Signs, Language, and Behavior* (New York: Prentice-Hall, 1946; New York: George Braziller, 1955), pp. 198–204. The present statement amplifies the position taken there in the light of recent developments. For an earlier statement of some of the value issues which are involved, see Charles Morris, *The Open Self* (New York: Prentice-Hall, 1948), Chap. 6.

[2] 'Mental illness' is a very vague and ambiguous term. In what follows we shall be thinking primarily of disturbances of the symbolic processes. Lawrence S. Kubie regards the neurotic process as a "distortion of symbolic function." See his "Social Forces and the Neurotic Process," in *Explorations in Social Psychology*, Alexander H. Leighton, John A. Clausen, and Robert N. Wilson, eds. (New York: Basic Books, 1957), p. 97. A recent study speaks of aphasia in similar terms: Charles E. Osgood and Murray S. Miron, eds., *Approaches to the Study of Aphasia* (Urbana, Ill.: University of Illinois Press, 1963).

under certain unusual circumstances "experimental neuroses" can be induced in animals. But in the main, under normal circumstances, man is the only symbolically sick animal. The signs that mark his power are also major sources of his distress.

George Mead was concerned with sign processes as they operate in the normal development of persons engaged in interpersonal activities. Harry Stack Sullivan,[3] conversant with Mead's general orientation, was concerned with the difficulties that persons encounter in such interpersonal activities. The social interactional approach to personality disturbances has proved very important.

A central villain in human life is anxiety. When a person is thwarted in social interaction (or in interaction with nonsocial objects), aspects of the situation become negatively appraisive and prescriptive signs. They awaken anxiety and inhibit action that might lead to satisfaction. These effects are in turn transferred to linguistic and postlinguistic signs of the anxiety-producing situation. Thus the individual is caught in a sign net:[4] he is prevented by his signs from acting in a way that might correct the signification of his signs through showing that the situation no longer has the characteristics signified. He is also prevented from acting in a way that might change the situation so that it no longer is anxiety-producing

Psychotherapy is to a large extent a process in which the unwarranted negatively appraisive and prescriptive aspects of certain signs are removed and are replaced by signs with positive appraisive and prescriptive significations. Psychotherapy is to this degree a learning process that changes the significations (and hence the interpretants) of certain signs, and especially signs that have evoked anxiety.

The change in the signification of signs, and thus in the person's tendencies to act in certain ways toward certain objects or situations, may be attempted in a number of ways.

---

[3] H. S. Sullivan, *The Interpersonal Theory of Psychiatry*, H. S. Perry and M. L. Gawel, eds. (New York: W. W. Norton, 1953).

[4] See Gregory Bateson, Don P. Jackson, Jay Haley, and John Weakland, "Toward a Theory of Schizophrenia," *Behavioral Science* 1 (1956), pp. 251–264. Bateson and his co-workers here explore one instance of this situation, namely where the individual in social interaction is presented by other individuals with signs that contradict each other in appraisive and prescriptive signification.

First, the technique used may rely primarily on the communications of therapist and patient. Dr. Jurgen Ruesch has taken as his central task the analysis of communication in relation to psychotherapy. His important work has extended over many years and has resulted in many articles and in three major books: *Communication: The Social Matrix of Psychiatry* (written with Gregory Bateson); *Disturbed Communication;* and *Therapeutic Communication*.[5] Disturbances requiring the psychotherapist are seen as disturbances of communication, and the task of the psychotherapist is seen as the restoration of communication. The analysis supporting this position does justice to the place of signs, values, and personality differences in communication and its disorders.

Second, the techniques of psychotherapy may utilize verbal behavior without being primarily in the form of conversation, as in the approach through learning theory. Reference may be made here to the work of Dr. Joseph Wolpe.[6]

Among other techniques used, Dr. Wolpe arranges a list of the situations in order of their increasing power to invoke anxiety in a given individual. Dr. Wolpe, starting from the least anxiety-producing situation, asks the patient (whose eyes are closed) to imagine such a situation as it is described, and to raise his finger the moment he experiences anxiety. The patient has been previously relaxed, possibly by hypnosis or possibly by E. Jacobson's methods. This relaxation reduces the anxiety concerning the

---

[5] These books were published by W. W. Norton & Co., New York, in 1951, 1957, and 1961. Dr. Ruesch has also written a book with Weldon Kees, called *Nonverbal Communication* (Berkeley, Calif.: University of California Press, 1956).

In *Disturbed Communication*, Dr. Ruesch gives the personality disturbance analogues for the present author's ways to live (pp. 223-224), and the disturbances possible for preferences of the main types of discourse presented in *Signs, Language, and Behavior* (pp. 251-253). In *Therapeutic Communication* (p. 123) Ruesch writes: "The therapist's operations are essentially symbolic in nature. He either speaks, gestures, or listens."

[6] Joseph Wolpe, *Psychotherapy by Reciprocal Inhibition* (Stanford, Calif.: Stanford University Press, 1958).

For further references and articles from this and similar points of view, see the journal *Behaviour Research and Therapy* (Oxford: Pergamon Press). The first issue (1963) contains a general article by J. Wolpe: "Psychotherapy: The Nonscientific Heritage and the New Science" (pp. 23-28).

situation described by Dr. Wolpe. In our terms (not Dr. Wolpe's), the technique eventually reduces or eliminates the negative appraisive and negative prescriptive aspects of the words employed by Dr. Wolpe, and hence the negative and prescriptive aspects of the situations described by these symbols. In the course of therapy this technique is applied step by step from the situations least provocative of anxiety to those most provocative of anxiety.

Third, the techniques used may dispense with verbal communication and rely upon changes made in the environment by the therapist. A case in which anxiety is not the problem can be illustrated by a study made by T. Agyllon.[7]

A psychotic patient who weighed over 250 pounds for many years refused to eat a special diet prescribed for her. She stole food from other patients and from the food counter. Methods of persuasion and coaxing were used, but they were not effective and were discontinued. The patient was then assigned a table of her own, and she was taken from the dining room whenever she went to a table not her own or attempted to steal food from the counter. The result was that the patient missed a part (or all) of her food whenever she attempted to steal food. Under this procedure the stealing response was eliminated in two weeks, and her weight steadily dropped until it became stabilized at 180 pounds. 'Stealing food' had been an appraisive and prescriptive symbol of getting more food; with the changed physical condition it came to signify receiving less food and so lost its former positive appraisive and prescriptive force.

Fourth, the techniques may utilize drugs. A person whose anxiety is lessened by such means may explore situations that were previously forbidding, and may come to find that former appraisals and prescriptions were unwarranted. This use of drugs is related to Dr. Wolpe's use of relaxation or mild hypnosis in order to help the patient experience without anxiety something that had previously provoked anxiety. This technique is seldom used in isolation.

In these various ways symbolic disturbances may be lessened or overcome. To the extent that this is so, the meanings of the dis-

---

[7] T. Agyllon, "Intensive Treatment of Psychotic Behaviour by Stimulus Satiation and Food Reinforcement," *Behaviour Research and Therapy* 1 (1963), pp. 53–61.

turbed person's signs are changed. His values are also changed in this process, if only in the minimal sense that different courses of behavior may be developed which are more effective in attaining the values he holds. In personality disturbances, as in all human behavior, signs and values interact in important ways.

Increasing attention is being paid to the topic of value in psychiatric theory and practice. This concern covers both the values of therapists and the values of persons with personality disturbances.[8]

The latter aspect of the problem was the subject of a pilot study I made with Dr. Bernice Eiduson and Dr. Denis O'Donovan, reported in a 1960 paper entitled "Values of Psychiatric Patients."[9] Here the ways-to-live questionnaire was given to 50 noninstitutionalized psychiatric patients, to the 50 spouses (or closest friends) of these patients, and to a control group of 50 normal persons. The 50 psychiatric patients had been diagnosed according to common psychiatric categories. For each patient a measure of the degree of severity of his disturbance was obtained, as well as a measure of the degree of value conflict as expressed in his ratings of the thirteen ways to live.

The various subgroups of patients (hysterics, obsessive-compulsives, passive-aggressives, schizophrenics, etc.) were found to show in their rating of the ways-to-live differences in the values they held which corresponded closely with the personalities and modes of behavior associated by psychiatrists with the various groups of personality disturbances.

It was reasonable to expect that the severity of the disturbance in the psychiatric patients would be related to the degree of difference in their values from those of their spouses. This expectation was not borne out to any marked degree by our data. In general, the values of married persons were found not to differ greatly from the values of their spouses as revealed by the ratings of the

---

[8] See Donald D. Glad, *Operational Values in Psychotherapy* (New York: Oxford University Press, 1959); Georgene H. Seward, "The Relation between Psychoanalytic School and Value Problems in Therapy," *American Journal of Psychoanalysis* 22, pp. 1-12; Charlotte Buhler, *Values in Psychotherapy* (New York: The Free Press of Glencoe, 1962).

[9] Charles Morris, Bernice T. Eiduson, Denis O'Donovan, "Values of Psychiatric Patients," *Behavioral Science* 5 (1960), pp. 297-312.

ways to live, and the extent of such differences did not significantly relate to the degree of disturbance in the married partner. There was some tendency for the patient's disturbance to be more severe if his spouse was high on Factor A (social control and self-restraint). But this tendency was not very marked.[10]

It also seemed reasonable to expect that the degree of severity of the patient's disturbance would be greater the more his values differed from the average values in his culture, but this expectation also was not borne out by the data. Differences of individual values from group values do not in themselves seem to lead to personality disturbances that require psychiatric help.

It was found, however, that the degree of severity of personality disturbance varied positively with the extent of value conflicts within the person. Thus a person who valued highly both dominance over persons and detachment from persons would certainly have problems in the attainment of both values. The conflict would be even greater if the person also positively valued dependence on persons.

Psychiatric patients in this study did not differ as a group very much in the order of their preferences for the thirteen ways to live from the order of preferences by other persons in the same culture. The psychiatric patients do not in general repudiate the values of their culture. They are, for the most part, simply having difficulties in achieving these values. It seems that the disturbed patients' ways to live are distorted, inefficient, and hence unsatisfying versions of the same ways of life for normal persons. The difference is not essentially in the conceived values but in the failure to make them operative values.

The purpose of these remarks has not been to maintain specific theses but to illustrate that in the study of persons in distress we are forced to pay more attention to the ways that signs and values function and interact in the behavior of such persons. Here, as elsewhere in the study of human behavior, the theory of signs and the theory of values are indispensable allies.

The difficulties encountered in the relation of persons also

---

[10] The patients with severe marital problems did differ in important respects from the patients without severe marital problems. These differences are described in the article under discussion.

appear in the relation between social groups within a culture or in the relation between cultures. Thus in the interaction of groups an underlying anxiety in each group relative to the other may provoke and sustain symbols that have a predominantly negative appraisive and prescriptive signification, and this anxiety in turn makes it difficult to change or correct the signification of the signs that each group uses with respect to the other. That the phenomenon has essential sign characteristics is shown by the way in which American symbols of Russia, Germany, and Japan have drastically changed over short intervals of time. The peoples by and large have not changed to the degree that their symbolization has changed.

Individual persons and social groups are human because of their symbol systems, and yet these symbols impose in turn heavy burdens on individual and social action. Man lives in his symbols, but he often maims himself, and even dies, because of them.

In this study we have hardly entered into man's rich symbolic life. We have been concerned mostly with the language needed to talk about this realm, and with the potentialities of a behaviorally grounded semiotic and axiology to explore it. The symbolic life of man has long been under study. It is the high merit of the workers in humanistic activities to have helped build this life, and the high merit of the students of the humanities to have kept this life before us in all its range and complexity. Such activity and such scholarship have been, and will remain, indispensable.

Attention to man's actions, his signs, and his values is no new enterprise. The more explicit behavioral orientation of the contemporary behavioral sciences is but a continuation in modern scientific form of an ancient tradition. It provides one more wedge for entering into the tissue of man's symbolic life. It holds the promise that behavioral scientists and scholars of the humanities will come to recognize that they are working in a common enterprise—the understanding and the strengthening of human signs so that human values may be enhanced.

Bibliography

Agyllon, T. "Intensive Treatment of Psychotic Behaviour by Stimulus Satiation and Food Reinforcement." *Behaviour Research and Therapy* 1 (1963), pp. 53-61.

Albert, Ethel M., and Clyde Kluckhohn. *A Selected Bibliography on Values, Ethics, and Esthetics.* Glencoe, Ill.: The Free Press, 1959.

Anshen, Ruth Nanda (ed). *Freedom, Its Meaning.* New York: Harcourt Brace & Co., 1940.

—— (ed.). *Language: An Enquiry into Its Meaning and Function.* New York: Harper & Bros., 1957.

Bar-Hillel, Y. "An Examination of Information Theory." *Philosophy of Science* 22 (1955), pp. 86-103.

Bateson, Gregory, Don P. Jackson, Jay Haley, and John Weakland. "Toward a Theory of Schizophrenia." *Behavioral Science* 1 (1956), pp. 251-264.

Berlyne, Daniel. "Knowledge and Stimulus-Response Psychology." *Psychological Review* 61 (1964), pp. 245-254.

Bloomfield, Leonard. "Linguistic Aspects of Science." *International Encyclopedia of Unified Science,* Vol. 1, No. 4. Chicago: University of Chicago Press, 1939.

Boulding, K. E. *The Image: Knowledge in Life and Society.* Ann Arbor, Mich.: University of Michigan Press, 1956.

Brown, Roger. *Words and Things.* Glencoe, Ill.: The Free Press, 1958.

—— and Don E. Dulaney. "A Stimulus-Response Analysis of Language and Meaning." In Paul Henle (ed.), *Language, Thought, and Culture.*

Buhler, Charlotte. *Values in Psychotherapy.* New York: The Free Press of Glencoe, 1962.

Carnap, Rudolf. "Empiricism, Semantics, and Ontology." *Revue Internationale de Philosophie* 11 (1950), pp. 208-228. Reprinted in Rudolf Carnap, *Meaning and Necessity,* pp. 205-221.

———. "Meaning Postulates." *Philosophical Studies* 3 (1952), pp. 65–73. Reprinted in Rudolf Carnap, *Meaning and Necessity*, pp. 222–229.

———. "On Some Concepts of Pragmatics." *Philosophical Studies* 6 (1955), pp. 89–91. Reprinted in Rudolf Carnap, *Meaning and Necessity*, pp. 248–250.

———. *Meaning and Necessity*, enlarged edition. Chicago: University of Chicago Press, 1956.

Carroll, John B. *The Study of Language*. Cambridge, Mass.: Harvard University Press, 1953.

———. Review of Osgood's *The Measurement of Meaning*. *Language* 35 (1959), pp. 58–77.

Cherry, Colin. *On Human Comunication: A Review, a Survey, and a Criticism*. Cambridge, Mass.: The Technology Press of the Massachusetts Institute of Technology; New York: John Wiley & Sons, 1957.

Chomsky, Noam. *Syntactic Structures*. The Hague: Mouton & Co., 1957.

Cronbach, A. *The Realities of Religion*. New York: Bookman Associates, Inc., 1957.

Dewey, John. *Experience and Nature*. Chicago: Open Court Publishing Co., 1925.

———. *Logic: The Theory of Inquiry*. New York: Henry Holt & Co., 1938.

——— and others. *Creative Intelligence*. New York: Henry Holt & Co., 1917.

Duncan, Hugh Dalziel. *Communication and Social Order*, second edition. Totowa, N.J.: Bedminster Press, 1956.

Feigl, Herbert. "Mind-Body, Not a Pseudoproblem." S. Hook (ed.), *Dimensions of Mind*, pp. 33–44.

Foerster, Heinz von (ed.). *Cybernetics: Transactions of the Eighth Congress*. New York: Macy Foundation, 1952.

Frank, Philipp (ed.). *The Validation of Scientific Theories*. Boston: The Beacon Press, 1954.

Frankena, W. K. " 'Cognitive' and 'Non-Cognitive'." In Paul Henle (ed.), *Language, Thought, and Culture*, pp. 146–172.

Frisch, Karl von. *Bees, Their Vision, Chemical Senses, and Language*. Ithaca, N.Y.: Cornell University Press, 1950.

Gendlin, Eugene T. *Experiencing and the Creation of Meaning*. New York: The Free Press of Glencoe, 1962.

Glad, Donald D. *Operational Values in Psychotherapy.* New York: Oxford University Press, 1959.

Goodenough, Ward H. "Componential Analysis and the Study of Meaning." *Language* 32 (1956), pp. 195–216.

Goss, Albert E. "Early Behaviorism and Verbal Mediating Responses." *American Psychologist* 16 (1961), pp. 285–298.

Greenberg, Joseph. *Essays in Linguistics.* Chicago: University of Chicago Press, 1957.

Grinker, Roy R. (ed.). *Toward a Unified Theory of Human Behavior.* New York: Basic Books, 1956.

Henle, Paul (ed.). *Language, Thought, and Culture.* Ann Arbor, Mich.: University of Michigan Press, 1958.

Hjelmslev, Louis. *Prolegomena to a Theory of Language.* Revised translation by Francis J. Whitfield. Madison, Wisc.: University of Wisconsin Press, 1961.

Hoijer, Harry (ed.). *Language in Culture.* Chicago: University of Chicago Press, 1954.

Hook, S. (ed.). *Dimensions of Mind.* New York: Collier Books, 1961.

Hull, Clark L. *A Behavior System.* New Haven: Yale University Press, 1952.

Hungerland, Isabel C. *Poetic Discourse.* University of California Publications in Philosophy, Vol. 33. Berkeley: University of California Press, 1958.

Jakobson, Roman. "Linguistics and Poetics." In T. A. Sebeok (ed.), *Style in Language,* pp. 350–377.

Jones, Lyle V., and Charles Morris. "Relations of Temperament to the Choice of Values." *Journal of Abnormal and Social Psychology* 53 (1956), pp. 345–349.

Kaplan, Abraham. "Referential Meaning in the Arts." *Journal of Aesthetics and Art Criticism* 12 (1954), pp. 457–474.

Kepes, Gyorgy. *The New Landscape in Art and Science.* Chicago: Paul Theobald & Co., 1956.

Kluckhohn, Clyde. "Value and Value-Orientations in the Theory of Action." In T. Parsons and E. A. Shils (eds.), *Toward a General Theory of Action,* pp. 388–433.

Kubie, Lawrence S. "Social Forces and the Neurotic Process." In A. H. Leighton, J. A. Clausen, and R. N. Wilson (eds.), *Explorations in Social Psychology,* p. 97.

Kuhn, Thomas S. "The Structure of Scientific Revolutions." *International Encyclopedia of Unified Science*, Vol. 2, No. 2. Chicago: University of Chicago Press, 1962.

Leighton, Alexander H., John A. Clausen, and Robert N. Wilson (eds.). *Explorations in Social Psychology*. New York: Basic Books, 1957.

Lepley, R. (ed.). *Value: A Cooperative Inquiry*. New York: Columbia University Press, 1949.

——— (ed.). *The Language of Value*. New York: Columbia University Press, 1957.

Lewis, Clarence I. *An Analysis of Knowledge and Valuation*. LaSalle, Ill.: Open Court Publishing Co., 1946.

———. *The Ground and Nature of the Right*. New York: Columbia University Press, 1955.

Lounsbury, Floyd G. "A Semantic Analysis of the Pawnee Kinship Usage." *Language* 32 (1956), pp. 158–194.

MacKay, Donald M. "In Search of Basic Symbols" and "The Nomenclature of Information Theory." In H. von Foerster (ed.), *Cybernetics: Transactions of the Eighth Congress*.

———. "Operational Aspects of Some Fundamental Concepts of Human Communication." *Synthese* 9, pp. 183–198.

Martin, Richard M. *Toward a Systematic Pragmatics*. Amsterdam: North-Holland Publishing Co., 1959.

———. *Intension and Decision*. Englewood Cliffs, N.J.: Prentice-Hall, 1963.

Mead, George H. "Scientific Method and Individual Thinker." In John Dewey and others, *Creative Intelligence*, pp. 176–227.

———. "Scientific Method and the Moral Sciences." *International Journal of Ethics* 33 (1923), pp. 229–247.

———. "The Nature of Aesthetic Experience." *Ethics* 36 (1926), pp. 384–387. Reprinted in part in G. H. Mead, *The Philosophy of the Act*, pp. 454–457.

———. "The Objective Reality of Perspectives." In A. Murphy (ed.), *The Philosophy of the Present*, pp. 161–175.

———. "The Limits of the Problematic." In G. H. Mead, *The Philosophy of the Act*, pp. 26–44.

———. *The Philosophy of the Act*. Charles W. Morris (ed.), with the collaboration of John M. Brewster, Albert M. Dunham, and David L. Miller. Chicago: University of Chicago Press, 1938.

Meyer, Leonard B. *Emotion and Meaning in Music.* Chicago: University of Chicago Press, 1956.

Moore, George E. *Principia Ethica.* Cambridge, England: Cambridge University Press, 1903.

Morris, Charles. "Semiotic and Scientific Empiricism." *Actes du Congrès International de Philosophie Scientifique—1935,* Vol. 1, pp. 2–16. Paris: Hermann et Cie, 1936. Reprinted in Charles Morris, *Logical Positivism, Pragmatism, and Scientific Empiricism,* pp. 56–71.

———. *Logical Positivism, Pragmatism, and Scientific Empiricism.* Paris: Hermann et Cie, 1937.

———. "Foundations of the Theory of Signs." *International Encyclopedia of Unified Science,* Vol. 1, No. 2. Chicago: University of Chicago Press, 1938.

———. "Esthetics and the Theory of Signs." *Journal of Unified Science (Erkenntnis)* 8 (1939), pp. 131–150.

———. "Science, Art, and Technology." *Kenyon Review* 1 (1939), pp. 409–423.

———. "The Mechanism of Freedom." In R. N. Anshen (ed.), *Freedom, Its Meaning.*

———. *Signs, Language, and Behavior.* New York: Prentice-Hall, 1946; George Braziller, 1955.

———. *The Open Self.* New York: Prentice-Hall, 1948.

———. "Axiology as the Science of Preferential Behavior." In R. Lepley (ed.), *Value: A Cooperative Inquiry,* pp. 211–222.

———. "Mysticism and Its Language." In R. N. Anshen (ed.), *Language: An Enquiry into Its Meaning and Function,* pp. 179–187. The paper, in a slightly shorter form, originally appeared in *Etc. A Review of General Semantics* 9 (1951), pp. 3–8.

———. "Man-Cosmos Symbols." In Gyorgy Kepes, *The New Landscape in Art and Science,* pp. 98–99.

———. "Significance, Signification, and Paintings." In R. Lepley (ed.), *The Language of Value.*

———. In Roy R. Grinker (ed.), *Toward a Unified Theory of Human Behavior,* pp. 350–351.

———. *Varieties of Human Value.* Chicago: University of Chicago Press, 1956.

———. "Words without Meaning" (review of B. F. Skinner's *Verbal Behavior*). *Contemporary Psychology* 3 (1958), pp. 212–214.

———. "Values, Problematic and Unproblematic, and Science." *Journal of Communication* 11 (1961), pp. 205–210.

———. See Jones, Lyle V., and Charles Morris.

———. See Osgood, Charles E., Edward E. Ware, and Charles Morris.

——— (ed.), with the collaboration of John M. Brewster, Albert M. Dunham, and David L. Miller. George H. Mead, *The Philosophy of the Act.* Chicago: University of Chicago Press, 1938.

———, Bernice T. Eiduson, and Denis O'Donovan. "Values of Psychiatric Patients." *Behavioral Science* 5 (1960), pp. 297–312.

——— and Daniel J. Hamilton. "Aesthetics, Signs, and Icons." To appear in *Journal of Philosophy and Phenomenological Research.*

——— and Lyle V. Jones. "Value Scales and Dimensions." *Journal of Abnormal and Social Psychology* 51 (1955), pp. 523–535.

——— and Frank Sciadini. "Paintings, Ways to Live, and Values." To appear in a series of volumes on the visual arts, edited by Gyorgy Kepes.

Mowrer, O. Hobart. *Learning Theory and the Symbolic Process.* New York: John Wiley & Sons, 1960.

Mukerjee, Radhakamal. *The Symbolic Life of Man.* Bombay: Hind Kitabs Ltd., 1959.

Murphy, A. (ed.). *The Philosophy of the Present.* LaSalle, Ill.: Open Court Publishing Co., 1932.

Osgood, Charles E., and Murray S. Miron (eds.). *Approaches to the Study of Aphasia.* Urbana, Ill.: University of Illinois Press, 1963.

——— and Thomas A. Sebeok (eds.). *Psycholinguistics.* Supplement to *International Journal of American Linguistics* 20 (1954).

———, George J. Suci, and Percy H. Tannenbaum. *The Measurement of Meaning.* Urbana, Ill.: University of Illinois Press, 1957.

———, Edward E. Ware, and Charles Morris. "Analysis of the Connotative Meanings of a Variety of Human Values as Expressed by American College Students." *Journal of Abnormal and Social Psychology* 62 (1961), pp. 62–73.

Parsons, Talcott. *The Social System.* Glencoe, Ill.: The Free Press, 1951.

———, Robert F. Bales, and Edward A. Shils. *Working Papers in the Theory of Action.* Glencoe, Ill.: The Free Press, 1953.

——— and E. A. Shils (eds.). *Toward a General Theory of Action.* Cambridge, Mass.: Harvard University Press, 1951.

Parsons, T., and E. A. Shils. "Values, Motives, and Systems of Action." In T. Parsons and E. A. Shils (eds.), *Toward a General Theory of Action.*

Pike, Kenneth L. *Language in Relation to a Unified Theory of the Structure of Human Behavior*, preliminary edition. Ann Arbor. Mich.: Wahr's University Bookstore, 316 South State Street. Part I, 1954; Part II, 1955; Part III, 1960.

Price, Kingsley Blake. "Is a Work of Art a Symbol?" *Journal of Philosophy* 50 (1953), pp. 485–503.

Quine, Willard Van Orman. *Word and Object.* Cambridge, Mass.: The Technology Press of the Massachusetts Institute of Technology; New York: John Wiley & Sons, 1960.

Rice, Philip Blair. *On the Knowledge of Good and Evil.* New York: Random House, 1955.

Richards, I. A. *Speculative Instruments.* Chicago: University of Chicago Press, 1955.

Ritchie, Benbow. "The Formal Structure of the Aesthetic Object." *Journal of Aesthetics and Art Criticism* 3 (1944), pp. 5–14.

Robinson, Edward Schouten. "The Languages of Sign Theory and Value Theory." In R. Lepley (ed.), *The Language of Value.*

Rossi-Landi, Ferruccio. *Significato, Comunicazione, e Parlare Comune.* Padova, Italy: Marsilio Editori, 1961.

Rudner, Richard. "On Semiotic Aesthetics." *Journal of Aesthetics and Art Criticism* 10 (1951), pp. 66–77.

Ruesch, Jurgen. *Disturbed Communication.* New York: W. W. Norton & Co., 1957.

———. *Therapeutic Communication.* New York: W. W. Norton & Co., 1961.

——— and Gregory Bateson. *The Social Matrix of Psychiatry.* New York: W. W. Norton & Co., 1951.

——— and Weldon Kees. *Nonverbal Communication.* Berkeley, Calif.: University of California Press, 1956.

Saussure, Ferdinand de. *Course in General Linguistics.* Translated from the fifth French edition by Wade Baskin. New York: Philosophical Library, 1959.

Sebeok, Thomas A. (ed.). *Style in Language.* Cambridge, Mass.: The Technology Press of the Massachusetts Institute of Technology; New York: John Wiley & Sons, 1960.

Seward, Georgene H. "The Relation between Psychoanalytic School and Value Problems in Therapy." *American Journal of Psychoanalysis* 22, pp. 1–12.

Seward, John P. "The Sign of a Symbol: A Reply to Professor Allport." *Psychological Review* 55 (1948), pp. 277–296.

Shannon, Claude, and Warren Weaver. *Mathematical Theory of Communication*. Urbana, Ill.: University of Illinois Press, 1949.

Staats, Arthur W. "Use of the Semantic Differential in Research on S-R Mediational Principles of Learning Word Meaning." Paper presented at Western Psychological Association, San Diego, California, April 1959.

Stevenson, Charles L. *Ethics and Language*. New Haven, Conn.: Yale University Press, 1944.

―――. "Symbolism in the Nonrepresentational Arts." In P. Henle (ed.), *Language, Thought, and Culture*, pp. 196–225.

―――. "Symbolism in the Representational Arts." In P. Henle (ed.), *Language, Thought, and Culture*, pp. 226–257.

Sullivan, H. S. *The Interpersonal Theory of Psychiatry*. H. S. Perry and M. L. Gawel (eds.). New York: W. W. Norton & Co., 1953.

Tate, Allen. *Reason in Madness*. New York: G. P. Putnam's Sons, 1941.

Taylor, Paul W. *Normative Discourse*. Englewood Cliffs, N.J.: Prentice-Hall, 1961.

Tinbergen, N. "The Evolution of Behavior in Gulls." *Scientific American*, 1960, pp. 118 ff.

von Foerster, Heinz. See Foerster, Heinz von.

von Frisch, Karl. See Frisch, Karl von.

Warner, Lloyd. *The Living and the Dead*. New Haven, Conn.: Yale University Press, 1959.

Wheelwright, Philip. *The Burning Fountain: A Study in the Language of Symbolism*. Bloomington, Ind.: Indiana University Press, 1954.

Wolpe, Joseph. *Psychotherapy by Reciprocal Inhibition*. Stanford, Calif.: Stanford University Press, 1958.

―――. "Psychotherapy: The Nonscientific Heritage and the New Science." *Behaviour Research and Therapy* 1 (1963), pp. 23–28.

Zuurdeeg, William F. *An Analytical Philosophy of Religion*. Nashville, Tenn.: Abingdon Press, no date given.

Index

Absolutist-relativist controversy 41–43
Action: signs in various phases of 21–22; three phases of 4–6; three requirements of 7–8
Aesthetic perception 73
Aesthetic sign: and value 69–72; as an icon 68–69
AGYLLON, T. 84
ALBERT, Ethel M. 34n
ALSOBROOK, James 53
Analytic implicates 13
Anxiety 82
A-ratings (appraisive ratings) 74
Art: and human behavior 79–80; experiments on 73–76; in relation to signs and values 65–80; is a work of art a sign? 67; relation of conceived and operative values in 77–79
Axiology: as the study of preferential behavior 17, 20

BALES, Robert F. 56
BAR-HILLEL, Y. 63
BARTLETT, George R. viii
BATESON, Gregory 82n
Behavior, preferential 16–17
BERGER, Fred R. viii
BERLYNE, Daniel 54
BLOOMFIELD, Leonard 62
BOULDING, Kenneth E. 34n
BROWN, Roger 50n
Buddhism 23
BUHLER, Charlotte 85n
BURKE, Kenneth 80n

CARNAP, Rudolf 33, 45, 46, 61n, 62
CARROLL, John B. 55, 61n

CASSIRER, Ernst 1, 15n
CHOMSKY, Noam 12n, 61n
'Cognitive': ambiguity of term 39n
Cognitivist-emotivist controversy 38–40
Communication 64
Complementary expectations (Parsons) 58–59
Comsign 59–60
Conceptual frameworks, and pragmatics 45–46
Context (of signs) 2
Contradictory implicates 14
CRONBACH, A. 34n

Dependence (or receptivity) 21–26
Detachment 21–26
DEWEY, John 6n, 16n, 19n, 26n
Discourse: formative 13–14; mathematical 14; mystical 14
Dominance 21–26
DULANEY, Don E. 50n
DUNCAN, Hugh Dalziel 58n

EIDUSON, Bernice T. 85
'Express': the term 10–11

FEIGL, Herbert 19n
Formators 11–13
FRANK, Philipp 46n
FRANKENA, W. K. 39n
FRISCH, Karl von 2

GENDLIN, Eugene T. 49n
GLAD, Donald D. 85n
GOODENOUGH, Ward H. 61n
Goss, Albert E. 50n
GREENBERG, Joseph 62

Index

HAMILTON, Daniel J. viii, 66n
HJELMSLEV, Louis 62
HOBBES, Thomas 81
HOIJER, Harry 61n
HULL, Clark L. 50n
HUME, David 32–33
HUNGERLAND, Isabel 33n

Information: selective and semantic 63–64
Information theory, a note concerning 62–64
Instrumental act 9
Interpretant 2, 3, 6; kinds of, and Osgood's meaning factors 54–56; nature of 49–52
Interpreters 2
Inquiry: appraisive 27; designative 27; evaluative versus nonevaluative 28; mathematical 27n; prescriptive 27; signs and values in 26–29

JACOBSON, E. 83
JAKOBSON, Roman 48n
JONES, Lyle V. 22n, 24n

KANT, Immanuel 32–33
KAPLAN, Abraham 10n, 67
KEES, Weldon 83n
KEPES, Gyorgy 80n
KLUCKHOHN, Clyde 19n, 34n
KUBIE, Lawrence S. 81n
KUHN, Thomas S. 46n

Lansign system 60–61
LEWIS, Clarence I. 20n, 37n
Linguistics 60–62
LOCKE, John 1
Logical empiricists 39
LOUNSBURY, Floyd G. 61n

MACKAY, D. M. 63–64
MARTIN, Richard M. 45
MEAD, George H. 4, 18n, 28n, 79–80, 82; on human mentality 29–31
Meaning 9–10; connotative (Osgood) 51–52
Meaning factors (Osgood) 52–56
MEYER, Leonard B. 34n, 68n
MIRON, Murray S. 81n
MOORE, George E. 34–36
MOWRER, O. Hobart 50n
MUKERJEE, Radhakamal 58n, 60n

"Naturalistic fallacy" 34–35
Norms: as unproblematic values 37

Object language: levels of signs in 13
Objective relativity 18
'Observable': the term 4n
O'DONOVAN, Denis viii, 85
OSGOOD, Charles E. 50–56, 61n, 81n
"Ought," the, and the "is" 36–38

PARSONS, Howard 10n
PARSONS, Talcott 56–60
PEIRCE, Charles 1, 33
PERRY, Ralph Barton, 16n
Personality disturbances 81–86
Philosophy: and pragmatics 44–47; contemporary views of 44
PIKE, Kenneth L. 61n
'Pragmatics' and pragmatism 44–45
Pragmatists 38
P-ratings (preference ratings) 74
Preferential behavior 16–17; and evaluative inquiry 29
PRICE, Kingsley Blake 66
Problematic, the, and its role in inquiry 28
Psychiatric patients, and values 85–86
Psychotherapy, and signs 82–83

QUINE, Willard V. O. 4n, 46n

Reflective thought (Mead) 30
Reinforcing property 8
Representational-mediational process 50–51
RICE, Philip Blair 40
RICHARDS, I. A. 33n
RITCHIE, Benbow 67n
ROBINSON, Edward Schouten 16n
ROSSI-LANDI, Ferruccio 34n
RUDNER, Richard 66
RUESCH, Jurgen 83

SAUSSURE, Ferdinand de 62
SCIADINI, Frank viii, 75n, 78
SEBEOK, T. A. 33n, 61n
Self-inclusive and self-exclusive points of view 29–30
Semantic differential 50–54
Semiosis (or sign process) 2
Semiotic: its scope 1; the basic terms of 2–3
SEWARD, Georgene H. 85n

SEWARD, John P. 50n
SHANNON, Claude 62–64
SHELDON, W. H. 76
SHILS, Edward A. 56
SHIRBROUN, B. Wayne viii
Sign 2; appraisive 4, 6; designative 4, 5, 6; formal 11–13; iconic 68–69; prescriptive 4, 5, 6
Signal 64–65
Significant symbol (Mead) 30
Signification 2, 3; appraisive 35; dimensions of 3–6; formative 11–14
Signs: lexical 11; metalinguistic 13; prelinguistic, linguistic, and postlinguistic 58; uses of 14–15
SKINNER, B. F. 3n, 20n
Social groups, conflict of, in terms of signs and values 87
Social sciences, and semiotic and axiology 56–62
Social system 57–60
STAATS, Arthur W. 55
STEVENSON, Charles L. 40n, 67, 72
Stimulus property 8
Stoicism 23
SUCI, George J. 50n
SULLIVAN, Harry Stack 82
Synsigns 12
System: cultural 57; social 57–60; the human action 57; three aspects of 20–21

TANNENBAUM, Percy H. 50n
TATE, Allen 70
TAYLOR, Paul W. 33n, 42–43
THURSTONE, L. L. 76
TINBERGEN, N. 64

Value: conceived 19; object 20; operative 19; the concept of 16–17
Value conflicts, and degree of severity of personality disturbances 86
Value factors A, B, C, D, and E 24–26
Value situation 18
Values: and preferential behavior 17–19; as objectively relative 18; primary—dependence, dominance, and detachment 21–23; primary, individual and social forms of 23–26; social and individual 17–18
VON FRISCH, Karl, see Frisch, Karl von

WARE, Edward E. 56
WARNER, Lloyd 58n
WEAVER, Warren 62
WEIGHT, Evelyn viii
WHEELWRIGHT, Philip 33n
WOLPE, Joseph 83–84

ZUURDEEG, W. F. 33n

www.ingramcontent.com/pod-product-compliance
Lightning Source LLC
Chambersburg PA
CBHW022108160426
43198CB00008B/394